PATH FOR WORDS

www.mascotbooks.com

Path for Words: Five-Minute Language Learning Activities for Children Ages One to Three Years

All content provided by Pixi Girl LLC dba Path for Words and this text is provided for informational purposes only for use by trained professionals and trained caregivers. The content is not intended to replace medical advice or consultation with the child's pediatrician or other medical professional. If you have concerns about your child's health or development, please communicate with your child's physician. If your child is currently receiving developmental therapies, please follow your child's individual treatment plan and your early intervention team's recommendations. All activities described by Path for Words require close supervision of the child by an adult within arm's reach of the child with eyes directly on the child. Some suggested activities may be hazardous and not appropriate for some children. Accordingly, good judgment based on the individual child is warranted. All content is provided as is without any warranty. Path for Words and the publisher assume no liability for accident or injury to persons or property resulting from your use of content provided by Path for Words.

For more information, please contact:
Mascot Books, an imprint of Amplify Publishing Group
620 Herndon Parkway, Suite 220
Herndon, VA 20170
info@mascotbooks.com

Library of Congress Control Number: 2024927706

CPSIA Code: PRV0525A

ISBN-13: 979-8-89138-175-9

Printed in the United States

This book is dedicated to the extraordinary families I have had the privilege of working with over the years. Your unwavering commitment to your children's success has been a driving force in the creation of this work, and your passion continues to inspire me both as a professional and as a parent.

PATH FOR WORDS

Five-Minute Language Learning Activities for Children Ages 1–3 Years

MARIE MARTINEZ

CONTENTS

PART I

GETTING STARTED ON YOUR CHILD'S PATH FOR WORDS .... **ix**

Introduction xi

1. Developmental Milestones 1
2. Bilingual and Multilingual Families 23
3. Concerning Behaviors 33
4. Making the Most of Speech and Language Sessions 57

PART II

SPEECH AND LANGUAGE ACTIVITIES **73**

5. How to Use These Activities 75
6. Bath Time 93
7. Diaper Changes 113
8. Snack Time 125
9. Restaurants 135
10. Outside Play 149
11. Books 163

Putting It All Together 173

Notes 177

About the Author 183

PART I

GETTING STARTED ON YOUR CHILD'S PATH FOR WORDS

INTRODUCTION

There never seems to be enough time—time for work, time for play, time to take care of yourself and your family, time to clean the house. The list is endless.

And once you become a parent or caregiver to a little one, time management becomes even more complex. Your priorities turn upside down. Your worldview shifts. You want to have input on everything your kiddo is exposed to. You spend all the time you can building your relationship with them, teaching them, loving them. And still, there's not enough time.

Throughout my years working as a dually certified speech-language pathologist and behavior analyst, I've often heard caregivers say, "I want to optimize the time I have with him, but I'm a working parent, and he's in day care for most of the day. I just don't have the time to sit down with him and do flash cards while I have dinner on the stove, and then it's bath time and then bedtime. When am I supposed to help him learn to communicate?"

Believe me, I understand. Not only because of all the families I've worked with throughout my career, but because I am a mother, too. You and I are kindred spirits. We both want the best for our children and are willing to lose sleep over it. But we've found out through experience that there's no changing the twenty-four-hour clock. And I'm happy to report that you don't have to magically conjure more hours in the day to help your child learn to communicate effectively.

We need to focus on improving the *quality* of the time we have together rather than trying to find *more* time in the day. We can enhance the quality of the learning opportunities, which don't require a classroom environment at all (no flash cards!). It's just you and your kiddo, communicating in your own home, in whatever way works best for you.

This book was designed to capitalize on the time you already spend with your child, such as during bath time and diaper changes, to turn everyday caregiving rituals into quality moments of language learning.

Over the past fifteen years, I've worked with many families in clinics, homes, and different community spaces. The strategies and concepts you'll learn here are the ones I have used with families throughout my career. I'll share the resources I've used, both in sessions and as a parent. This book will help you learn more about your children's individual communication skills and how to enhance their complexity—in less than five minutes at a time.

Enjoy taking your child on their path for words!

My Story

My favorite thing in the world is hearing a child say their first word and witnessing their parents' reaction. If that word happens to be "mom" or "dad," that's the cherry on top. Sometimes, it's simply an "mmm" sound as the child reaches up toward Mom. We often work hard toward this goal, so "mmm" is just as exciting as hearing "Mom." I typically work with children who have learning differences, such as developmental delay, global delay, language delay, and autism spectrum disorder (ASD). No matter the label, each child is an individual. Because of these learning differences, caregivers and children may have worked very hard to get to that first communication, making it all the more impactful to witness. Depending on the child's verbal level and developmental abilities, this first communication may be nonverbal, such as a reach, a point, or the use of a visual cue such as a picture of an object they'd like to play with. Whatever the communication happens to be, and no matter how hard we had to work to get there, I always think, *I love my job*.

I never intended to become a speech-language pathologist (SLP) or a behavior analyst (BA). When I was in high school, I was a singer and a cheerleader and experienced what is known as "vocal abuse" (the technical term for overusing our vocal cords). I went to see a voice therapist and noticed all the kids in the waiting room. I wasn't expecting to see kids! The main focus of my therapy was speech, so the SLP and I spent hours over the next several weeks just talking while she provided me with rehabilitation on my vocal cords. This included exercises and speaking strategies that would allow me to continue my lifestyle in a healthy way. Throughout our therapy sessions, I witnessed the way she lit up when speaking about the families she'd served and the different diagnoses and individualized treatments she described. I knew I'd enjoy the work just as much as she did.

As an undergraduate, I studied communication disorders at Purdue University. During that time, I had the opportunity to focus my studies on teaching individuals with complex communication needs and augmentative and alternative communication (AAC). I had a psychologist friend who specialized in behavioral issues. She was finishing her PhD and working with a two-year-old child diagnosed with an ASD. She was moving out of the state for a new job and asked me if I'd like a referral to work with this family. I barely knew what autism was at that point, but I trusted her and accepted the referral. I talked to the family on the phone, telling them that I didn't have much experience in behavior, but I was interested to know how their child's SLP and behavioral team were teaching him to use AAC and how the SLP and BA worked together to help their sweet two-year-old.

This family changed my life. (That two-year-old child is now in high school, and we're all still in touch.) I got to see the real-time impact of early intervention through my learning experience with this family. The SLP and BA worked beautifully together. They communicated regularly via email, phone, and in person when able to create the ideal communication plan for this child. This type of collaboration is unique, and being in the field, this made an impact on the next steps of my career.

After completing my master's degree in speech-language pathology, I did a clinical fellowship at Vanderbilt University Medical Center. There, I worked under an SLP and a behavioral analyst who worked together to create language programs for a research project focused on interventions for young children with ASD. Vanderbilt offered me an introduction to the world of research and bridging the gap between research and clinical practice.

Speech-language pathology is a fantastic mix of evidence-based research, guiding children on their path for words, new communication skills, empathy, and problem-solving. Plus, I love children, and I can't think of anything more rewarding than helping to deepen their relationships with their caretakers through progress in communication. Not only do their relationships with their caretakers deepen through language, but also their relationships to the world as a whole.

Early Intervention

I've had the opportunity to work with many families throughout my fifteen years in practice. While each child is different, I've seen a large number of children whose communication could've been significantly improved with early intervention. However, many caregivers don't know what signs to look for to determine if their child could benefit from speech, language, and communication interventions that would help them continue to grow at a developmentally appropriate pace.

Many families who *do* try to speak to a provider about it are often advised to wait it out. I have completed countless speech and language assessments with school-aged children presenting communication differences, whose caregivers reported knowing something was different by the age of two, but a family member or even a health-care provider advised them to "wait and see."

I wish health-care professionals and well-meaning families would consider this phrase more carefully before using it. This is in no way meant to discredit what providers say otherwise, but we have to keep in mind that most providers only have a few minutes to spend with each child every few months. It's almost impossible to have a real handle on a person's speech and language progress with such limited face-to-face time. Six months is a *long* time when it comes to speech and language development. During the time between provider visits, if the problem *didn't* resolve, that child could be significantly behind in their communication.

That doesn't even touch on the stress and turmoil that can occur in the homes of families whose children are struggling to communicate. It's frustrating not to be understood, and for a toddler who has had very little time to learn how to communicate in a safe and effective way, especially if they also have a learning difference, this frustration can turn into a concerning behavior. Now instead of teaching a foundational skill, we're having to work through fraught emotions, often on the part of the child and caregivers alike.

Preventive measures are my main area of interest and the reason the Path for Words program was created. If a caregiver has access to strategies that they can use when their child is one-year-old or younger, it gives the child a huge advantage compared with not getting these strategies until they are school-aged. It's important to note that the strategies in this book are not intended to entirely prevent a speech and language disorder. Having access to these strategies could improve your child's complexity of communication, regardless of whether they have a speech and language disorder.

The strategies can also help you recognize instances of communication at a child's different verbal levels: preverbal, verbal 1, verbal 2, and verbal 3. (These levels are loosely based on the Hanen Centre's *More Than Words*,[1] but for the purpose of this book, these labels are not meant to be "categories" per se but rather to identify communication goals and next steps.) We'll discuss these levels (instead of ages, as the verbal levels don't always correspond neatly with age) at length later in the book. These strategies can also help you notice if your child isn't meeting milestones and could benefit from speech and language services. If you do need to work with an SLP, this book will provide you with a framework to communicate with your child's team regarding the goals you have for your child and the goals they are developing.

Whether it comes from the parent of one of my patients, a friend, or the back of my mind, there's one question I hear more than any other: "Is there something else I should be doing?" The truth is, there's no one-size-fits-all answer. Each kiddo is different, and families have different levels of needs and available time. In this book I try to provide as many detailed answers to this question as possible, and by integrating the strategies into existing day-to-day activities, I aim to avoid adding one more task to your already busy lives. Believe me, as a working mom, I know the importance of optimizing the time we spend with our little ones.

Let's Dive In

After hearing what felt like the thousandth caregiver say, "I wish I had known this years ago," I started thinking of a tool I could give them that would equip them with the foundational skills I use in my work. I'm not expecting everyone to become an SLP—I very much want to keep my job! What I hope to accomplish through this resource is that by the time a child comes to my practice, the family will have already integrated these foundational practices into their day-to-day lives. This book introduces these practices, which I have broken down into step-by-step, easy-to-follow strategies you can do during bath time, diaper changes, and other activities you probably already do with your child on a daily basis. This book also helps you monitor your child's progress through milestones so you can bring them to see an SLP as early as possible if the need arises. I want to help put the tools in your toolbox so you can meet your child at their level of speech and language development. (What you *won't* have to do is buy new toys. I've worked in many opportunities to introduce safe household items rather than any new equipment.) This book should be helpful for anyone who serves as a caretaker for a toddler. Even if your child is a newborn, this book includes information about the upcoming stages of development that could help you in the near future.

Writing this book has been a goal of mine for many years. Becoming a mother during the process of writing it only solidified my commitment to empowering caretakers to take a proactive approach to their children's language learning and communication skills. If one of my future clients ever shows up with it in hand, having used it before they met me, I'll consider this entire endeavor a success.

Whether you obtained this book through my direct recommendation or you happened to pick it up, I hope you find the strategies helpful on your child's path for words journey.

One final note: no matter how many diplomas I've obtained in this field, I'll be the first to admit that (a) the research is always evolving, and (b) *you* know your child best. I encourage you to use your instincts. If your child hates bath time, feel free to skip the bath time chapter and the like. I'll also refer to additional resources throughout this text, and I encourage you to do your own research into the companies, books, and organizations I mention. I do not endorse any of these resources specifically. You know your family values and beliefs the best.

With that, let's dive right in. In chapter 1 we will learn about milestones: what they are, how we can use them, and one of the most important aspects of communication: gestures.[2]

CHAPTER 1

DEVELOPMENTAL MILESTONES

From the moment we find out we're going to become a parent, grandparent, or caregiver to a little one, we start to dream of the person they will become. We plan for everything we can think of to make their world safer and better than what we experienced growing up.

Of course, there are some things we can control to help them succeed, such as good nutrition, safety, comfort, love, and so on. Then there are things we mostly cannot control, such as genetics or how others will interact with and treat them. With both what we can and cannot control, all we can do is try our best to set them up for success.

Even though you can't control every aspect of your child's life, and we don't want to, their autonomy is important, you can monitor their development through milestones. The monitoring itself can create learning opportunities for your child and fun bonding activities for both of you. These developmental milestones can also point to emerging differences in your child's development that may warrant the attention of a pediatrician or speech-language pathologist (SLP).

In this chapter you'll gain an understanding of developmental milestones by age, starting at one year and ending at three years. We will discuss quick and easy ways to check a child's developmental progress toward communication milestones.

What Is a Developmental Milestone?

Developmental milestones are skills that "most" children develop at a particular age (months/years). Some children will develop these skills later; some will develop them earlier.

Here are some broad examples of developmental milestones (adapted from the PLS-5,[1] American Speech-Language-Hearing Association (ASHA) Identify the Signs,[2] and CDC Act Early[3] resources):

- A one-year-old understanding "What's that?" as a question and attempting to provide an answer.
- A one-year-old looking at you and laughing during play.
- A sixteen-month-old pointing at an airplane in the sky and looking at you to share that moment.
- A two-year-old putting two words together, such as "Mom, look," or "Dad, here!"
- A three-year-old asking, "Why?"

Communication milestones are not only important for social communication skills, self-advocacy, and development; they also lay the foundation of preliteracy skills.[4]

As commonly stated in education, "First, we learn to read, then we read to learn."

We can add onto that here and say, "First, we learn to communicate, then we learn to read."

Communication teaches children the speech sounds and language concepts that will help set them up for a successful reading career. When a caregiver reads to a child, the child becomes familiar with speech sounds, which is their first introduction to words. If a child is delayed at developing their speech sounds or has difficulty making that sound, it's harder for them to translate the sound to understand written words. (There are many books and resources about preliteracy if this interests you.)

Whether it's walking, talking, reading, or anything else, watching a child reach developmental milestones is one of the most rewarding experiences in many adults' lives. That's why parents often remember their child's first words or where they took their first steps. But recognizing developmental milestones serves a purpose other than sentimentality—missed milestones can alert a parent or caregiver to potential developmental differences, which might mean the child would benefit from an SLP's expertise. If your child has missed significant milestones two months in a row, or if you feel that your child is falling behind their peers developmentally, it's a good idea to consult with an expert. You know them best!

English-Speaking American Children

It's important to note that the developmental milestones discussed in this book and many of the additional resources

I mention are milestones for children born and raised in the United States who speak English as their first language. (See chapter 2 for multilingual resources.)

Speech and language milestones are specific to the language or languages a child is learning to speak. This surprises a lot of people!

For example, a child learning to speak English will, over time, learn to use different consonant sounds, than a child learning to speak Spanish will learn.

When I was consulting in an elementary school, one of the children we worked with had recently moved to the United States from Spain. When he was being assessed for a speech and language disorder, his therapist thought he might need intervention for a lisp. However, a lisp in Castilian Spanish is part of the dialect and is not a disorder. This kiddo was making all the consonant sounds he'd been regularly exposed to by this point in his life. The best language support for him was learning how to speak the English language, not being treated for disordered language. "Disordered" language[5] would have started for this child in Spanish, his first language.

Examples such as this exist throughout different languages, as each language has its own set of speech sounds, and each person has their own set of gestures and mannerisms when communicating. The way we learn to communicate in our native language is unique. For this reason, assessments and interventions should be uniquely created for each person. In this book you will read many different examples, and I encourage you to individualize each activity to fit your child's and family's strengths.

For this reason, when we assess speech and language skills in children who speak a language other than English as their first language, it is not recommended to use only English assessments to determine if there is a delay or disorder in language development.

Children with Disabilities or Developmental Differences

Imagine you arrive a bit early to pick up your child from day care. All the children are seated at the snack table. You have a moment to observe your child engaging with their peers. You notice the words the other children are using and how they communicate with one another. You haven't heard your child use those words yet. At that moment you think, *Hmm. Is he just shy?* Or, *It'll be okay. Maybe the peers are just advanced.* Maybe you don't initially think something is "different," even if it's clear your kiddo is at a different developmental level than their same-aged peers. Even if you have the time to look into the issue further, you may not think it's necessary.

It may not be necessary to dive deeper into your child's interactions with their peers. They may not have napped well, or they could have been upset or not themselves that day or during that routine.

This example is not meant to scare you or to diagnose your child from this one interaction. However, it is meant to empower you to get the conversation started with your child's pediatrician or care team as early as possible. The earlier you identify the supports your child may need, the earlier they can receive them.

People often have an image of what they want for their children. When something sticks out as a difference, it can be hard for some parents or caregivers to address it. Recognizing a difference in development does not mean that there is something "wrong" with your little one or that they need to be "fixed" with therapy. Recognizing a difference is an opportunity to help fill in gaps in development and provide the support your child needs as early as possible to progress in their individual best way for their future. We'll go into detail about how to do that throughout this book.

For parents and caregivers who already know your child has a developmental disability or speech/language disorder, this book can help you recognize gaps. It can also help you learn to meet your child at their level and build upon their strengths and existing skills.

For instance, if your two-year-old is only using vowel sounds, instead of thinking, *My child is two and should be using two-word phrases. Therefore, they should . . .*, you can focus on building on their strengths and current communication skills by adding consonants onto those vowels or adding gestures to the sounds, rather than specifically thinking about what the milestones say.

We're focusing on milestones early on as a form of awareness, but they should not be your primary focus. Your main focus should be building on the communicative strengths of your child and bonding communicatively together. This book will hopefully be able to help you identify your child's strengths regardless of their level of development.

The Importance of Teaching Gestures

A gesture is exactly what it sounds like: a purposeful body movement or action made to communicate a message. Pointing, waving, and shrugging are all examples of simple gestures.

Gestures can involve touch as well, such as giving a high five to a teammate on the baseball field who just hit a home run.

Toddlers learn to communicate by watching and listening to the words and gestures used by the adults around them. Then they try to imitate us to use "their version" of the words and gestures we used. Their version may only match ours in intonation or in the number of syllables, depending on their verbal level. If they are speaking at a one- to two-word level, they will likely pick up only one word and a few gestures. This begins their path for words and effective and efficient communication. At least 70 percent of a message sent is through the use of gestures.[6]

The following are two considerations as to why we should teach toddlers early on how to use gestures to communicate:

1. **Gestures can lead to verbal language.**[7]
   For example, if you are outside with your toddler and you see an airplane fly overhead, you might point at it and say, "Airplane!" They put together that the object you're gesturing to has a name, and the more often this is repeated, the quicker they are likely to learn the word. This is called "mapping."[8] Sometimes, once a child learns that an adult will name an object when they point to it, they will have a lot of fun pointing at objects, people, or animals to hear new words. (If your child does not start to use their index finger to point for communication around one year of age, you will want to begin to teach them to do so.)

   This cycle continues until the child begins to make sounds paired with their pointing gesture that will sound similar to the word(s) the adult is using. They may even imitate exactly what the adult said. This entire language learning opportunity occurs because our child used a gesture (pointing) to communicate. As simple as a point may seem, when children do not use these gestures, it's harder for adults to provide language learning opportunities. Caregivers are often pulled in many different directions all at once. So a simple point toward a person, toy, or object can create a perfect, organic opportunity to teach and learn.

2. **Gestures are (usually) clear.**
   Sometimes, a toddler's message is hard to understand because they either don't have the right words, don't have any words yet, or their pronunciation is hard to decipher. Gestures are much easier to translate. I once worked with an eighteen-month-old who would walk up and say, "Pawa." When I didn't understand him, he would stomp and become upset. I had him "show" me what he was saying and led me over to the pantry. I started taking items off the shelf and labeling them for him. His mother was sitting actively involved in on our session, and she reached for the peanut butter jar. As soon as she touched it, his face lit up in a smile. We then taught him to take the peanut butter jar to his mom to communicate that he wanted a peanut butter snack by giving him a small amount (this was a snack, not his main source of nutrition), closing the jar, and setting it down in front of him. When he grabbed the jar and tried to open it, we immediately taught him to hand the jar to his mother while modeling, "peanut butter." We still labeled it for him, even though the words are not easy to say. Giving or handing a desired item to a caregiver is a very handy tool for a preverbal or nonverbal kiddo!

Not all gestures are universal, but most of the ones you'd be doing with a small child will be understood by many. The list of gestures in chapter 1 (pointing, handing objects, eye contact, etc.) is all simple and mostly universal. Gestures are an important first step in language development for many different children.

UNIVERSAL GESTURES VERSUS SIGN LANGUAGE[9]

Many caregivers want to teach American Sign Language (ASL) to their children, which could be a great option for some families. Some common signs to teach babies and preverbal toddlers are "more" and "all done." These very common signs aren't understood by non-ASL users the way a nod or a shake of the head would be universally understood. Especially for a child with a developmental difference, considering teaching universal gestures in addition to ASL may facilitate more language learning opportunities for a child.

Monitoring Milestones

Imagine you and your child are playing with a farm animal puzzle. You may think, *Well, I've labeled the same animals over and over, I've mooed, I've quacked . . . what else can I do?*

There are *many* other things you can do, and I've made it as simple as possible for you to figure out what's next. In the section below, you'll find several different ways to continue to enrich your play with your child.

I don't know about you, but I appreciate a little structure during play! Just a sprinkle of structure helps me know what I can do to help my kiddos build on their individual strengths and opportunities. I hope these activities help enrich your experience of playing with your child as much as they can help enrich your child's learning.

In the example above, you could look at the gestures chart below (Sixteen Months), which would suggest you ask your child to point to various animals or hand you specific puzzle pieces. The activities below can also help you know what to discuss with your child's pediatrician/care team during wellness checks.

Use the additional resources below to ensure that you're screening your child with a complete list of skills across domains while recognizing possible differences. This is not meant to be a complete assessment but rather a way for parents or caregivers to keep an eye on a child's progress at home and serve as a starting point for additional conversations with your child's care team, if needed.

TIP FOR SUCCESS

Try to assess your child's skills by engaging in activities they enjoy. Nobody wants to be judged while performing a task they dislike! Just like adults, children are in the best state for learning and skill growth when they're well rested, fed, and loved. If they are having an "off day" or don't feel their best, you can choose some of the simpler strategies from the daily routine chapters below instead. (That goes for you, too!)

(Please note that there are milestones before the age of one, but I have not included them in this book. To learn more about those milestones speak with your child's care team.)

Twelve Months (One Year)

At twelve months we're generally looking for a child to attend to learning opportunities, meaning they are watching and listening to you and others around them and attempting to "name" objects and people. Their "words" will most likely sound like word approximations and may not have all the sounds needed to complete a word. As long as they are trying to use sounds to label people or things, celebrate their communication attempts together!

TWELVE MONTHS (ONE YEAR)		
Skill	Learned/ Still Learning	
Follows the direction of your point to look at the item or person you named	L	SL
Says *at least* one word consistently and meaningfully *and* attempts to copy your sounds/words	L	SL
Looks up at you periodically during play, laughing and smiling while looking at you for at least one minute	L	SL

TWELVE MONTHS (ONE YEAR) *continued*		
Skill	Learned/ Still Learning	
Pauses or stops when you say, "No, stop," or similar phrases	L	SL
Responds to their name by looking, pausing, or turning when called	L	SL
Does not have tantrums that disrupt family daily life and calms when you comfort them	L	SL
Plays with toys as they are designed after being taught	L	SL
Uses gestures/speech to interact with you	L	SL
Notes		

**Adapted from the PLS-5, ASHA Identify the Signs, and CDC Act Early resources as of July 2024.*

Learned versus Still Learning

When does something count as "learned"? If your child is using this skill daily and easily with multiple people, it is "learned." If they've used it only once or twice or only with you, count it as "still learning." If you've never seen the behavior at all, leave it blank for now.

Sixteen Months

At sixteen months these gestures (communicative body actions) are **imperative for continued communication development**. Ensure that your child is regularly using these gestures paired with a sound or sound combination and eye contact. If they are not, discuss this with their pediatrician and practice teaching these gestures paired with eye contact and vocalization daily. These gestures lead to sustained and continued complexity in speech, language, and social development.

SIXTEEN MONTHS		
Skill	Learned/ Still Learning	
Points to different objects/people/actions and uses the pointer finger to their lips to indicate "shhhhh"	L	SL
Waves	L	SL
Shows objects	L	SL
Gives objects to you	L	SL
Uses gestures first while looking at you to start games (peekaboo, blowing kisses, clapping) and to communicate their needs/wants	L	SL
Dances	L	SL
Shakes head left and right and nods to communicate yes or no	L	SL
Reaches for items/people and raises their arms	L	SL

SIXTEEN MONTHS *continued*		
Skill	**Learned/ Still Learning**	
Points/taps to indicate a need or to get someone's attention	L	SL
Gestures specific to your family culture (i.e., high five, cheers, palms facing up/shrug to "say" where did it go, peace sign, thumbs-up)	L	SL
Notes		

**Adapted from the First Words Project and ASHA Identify the Signs.*

TO LEARN MORE

To learn more about the gestures at sixteen months, I recommend the resource "16 by 16" from First Words Project.[10]

Twenty-Four Months (Two Years)

At twenty-four months we're generally looking for a child to use one-word during interactions regularly and two-word combinations to describe events happening in their world, ask us for items/people they need, answer questions, and expand their vocabulary rapidly through books and play activities. At this age words may not be 100 percent clear. However, what they are communicating—using a combination of sounds, words, and gestures—can be understood by someone who may not know them well.

TWENTY-FOUR MONTHS (TWO YEARS)		
Skill	Learned/ Still Learning	
They are using the skills in the twelve- and sixteen-month gestures mentioned above	L	SL
Uses words to gain your attention (saying your name, "look," "hey," etc.)	L	SL
Uses words to label items/actions (dog, goldfish, cup, run, jump)	L	SL
Uses words to obtain items/actions (want, I want, help, a person's name, etc.)	L	SL
Uses words for repetition of a game or item (more, again, my turn, etc.)	L	SL
Answers yes/no questions	L	SL
Uses and understands at least fifty words for food, toys, animals, body parts, people, actions, places, and pronouns	L	SL
Combines two or more words, such as "Mommy, look"	L	SL
Follows two-step directions, such as "Get your cup and put it in the sink"	L	SL

TWENTY-FOUR MONTHS (TWO YEARS) *continued*		
Skill	Learned/ Still Learning	
Uses the consonant sounds *P*, *B*, *D*, *M*, and *H* appropriately at the beginning of words, such as *pat*, *daddy*, *horse*, *mommy*, and *bunny*	L	SL
Notices emotions (may react to others crying or laughing)		
Notes		

**Adapted from the PLS-5, ASHA Identify the Signs, and CDC Act Early resources.*

Thirty-Six Months (Three Years)

At thirty-six months we're generally looking for children to begin using more complex language, such as using negatives, action words, and plurals; learning new words rapidly during book reading and play; and using three-to-five-word sentences. At this age you should understand most of what they say even when they are using longer sentences.[11]

THIRTY-SIX MONTHS (THREE YEARS)		
Skill	Learned/ Still Learning	
They are using the skills in the twelve-, sixteen-, and twenty-four-month gestures mentioned above	L	SL
Points to actions in books or in pictures when you name them (e.g., eating, playing, sleeping)	L	SL
Understands negatives (e.g., no food, not in there)	L	SL
Uses plurals at the end of words (e.g., dogs, chips)	L	SL
Regularly labels objects/people/animals in books	L	SL
Does not have difficulty getting words out	L	SL
Uses three-word phrases, such as "I want juice" or "Look at me"	L	SL
Able to tell adults their name	L	SL
Speaks to children and adults	L	SL
Able to tell reasons for things (e.g., needing water because they are thirsty)	L	SL
Able to ask why, where, who, and how questions	L	SL
Able to answer function questions (e.g., reason we wear a jacket, use a spoon, go to bed)	L	SL

THIRTY-SIX MONTHS (THREE YEARS) *continued*		
Skill	**Learned/ Still Learning**	
Uses "-ing" and "-ed" forms (e.g., running, jumped)	L	SL
Has two back-and-forth verbal exchanges as a beginning conversation (Dad says, "Do you want a snack?" Child says, "I want goldfish." Day says, "We don't have goldfish." Child says, "Veggie straws?")	L	SL
Notes		

**Adapted from the PLS-5, ASHA Identify the Signs, and CDC Act Early resources.*

Developmental Screening Resources

If you're looking for resources to better understand your child's developmental skills, here are a few that you can use. If any of these skills are confusing or if you're unsure how to look for a specific skill, ask your child's pediatrician at their next wellness check or reach out to us on social media for examples. You can find us on Instagram @pathforwords and at our website, www.pathforwords.com.

Early Intervention State Agencies

There are government-provided early intervention agencies in each state. Each state is different; however, you can reach out to your state agency for screeners or to ask any questions. Intake processes may take several months, so the earlier you contact them, the better. They are only able to serve children up until a certain birthday. For that reason, if you contact them shortly before your child would "age out" of their services, they may only be able to help with a screening and by connecting you with the public school resources in your area. At that point your child's pediatrician will need to refer them for additional screenings or assessments.

This process can seem daunting, requiring calls to agencies, scheduling, dealing with waitlists, pediatrician appointments, referrals, and, once again, more waiting time. I have worked with families who have gone through this process and waited several months for services to begin because of scheduling issues, services available in their area, and provider turnover. Assume positive intent from the individuals in your area who are working hard to serve many families. Be in regular communication with them so you're both on the same page about waitlists and accessing the resources available to you.

One of the reasons why I wanted to write this book in the first place is to help you get a head start on your child's development and provide you with quick and easy strategies you can use now while you may be waiting for consistent support or want to ensure your child has a foundation for language success.

RESOURCES IN THE INTERIM

The time between noticing a gap or difference in your child's development and actually getting in front of a PCP or SLP can take several months. Don't try the "wait and see" approach. This book is designed to be a tool for you to use in the meantime so you don't miss out on valuable months (or even years) when you could be building on your child's communication skills.

These resources are freely available for caregivers to look at if they have concerns about their child's speech and language or if they want to learn more about their child's speech and language development. These are some great options that can help, especially if you are waiting on services and want to get started now.

Early Intervention Services:

Use this link below to locate the early intervention contact information specific for your state. You can also go directly to the US Centers for Disease Control and Prevention (CDC) to locate resources in your state.

Visit cdc.gov/FindEI.

Ages and Stages:

This is a general screener that may be administered by pediatricians and your state-provided early intervention staff.

Visit agesandstages.com.

Centers for Disease Control and Prevention:

There is a downloadable PDF document available, as well as an app you can use to track a child's developmental milestones across domains and talking points for discussions with a child's pediatrician/care team.

Visit cdc.gov/ncbddd/actearly.

American Speech-Language-Hearing Association:

This is a resource that includes developmental speech-language and feeding milestones. The feeding milestones checklists can be used with children who speak languages other than English and live in a country other than the United States.

Visit asha.org/public/developmental-milestones.

First Words Project:

The Baby Navigator can help screen your child for social communication skill development before the age of two.

Visit babynavigator.com/soco.

So far we've discussed milestones for English-speaking American children. In the next chapter, we will discuss children who are raised in bilingual or multilingual families and what that means for communication. Even if your child only speaks English, there are plenty of opportunities to explore the benefits of exposure to a second language, including learning how to be respectful of others' linguistic and cultural differences.

CHAPTER 2

BILINGUAL AND MULTILINGUAL FAMILIES

You might look at the title of this chapter and think, *Well, I only speak one language, so I'll skip this one!*

Don't turn the page so fast!

You don't have to be fluent in a second language to expose your child to basic multilingual skills and to appreciate other languages. If you've been teaching your child "baby signs" or the basics of American Sign Language (ASL), you have already exposed them to another language. That's right—sign language is a language in its own right. Some people don't realize that, but ASL has a unique set of grammatical rules and structure, just like any spoken language.

TO LEARN MORE

To learn more about ASL, here are a few resources you can explore:

- National Institute on Deafness and Other Communication Disorders[1]
- Gallaudet University (https://gallaudet.edu)—focused on the Deaf community
- A university in your area with coursework focused on ASL
- Government and religious organizations in your area that offer ASL interpretation services

It may come as a surprise that you don't have to speak another language fluently for your child to benefit from exposure to it.

In this chapter you'll learn about bilingualism/multilingualism and gain basic knowledge on the rationale behind exposing your child to all the languages your family speaks on a daily basis. If you're a monolingual family, this chapter will help you understand opportunities to learn a second language together.

The Benefits of Exposure to Languages

Some people worry that exposure to a second language will delay a child's language acquisition in their first language, but research does not support this idea.[2]

It will not harm your child's acquisition of English if your spouse, parent, or any other caregiver speaks another language around them regularly during their early developmental years.

In fact, early exposure to another language might help them learn that language later in life.[3] Infants' brains start to pick up on the sounds they hear regularly, such as being spoken to by a caregiver. Over time, they learn to pay attention to those sounds, and then those sounds turn into words they can understand.

Even if your child wasn't exposed to another language as an infant, there are still many opportunities to engage with other languages in your play and literacy activities. Language learning during the toddler years is so much fun (although I may be biased). Our kiddos are hungry for engaging play activities, and their brains are ready for us to fill them with fun literacy and language-rich activities. The first three years of life are full of opportunities for second language learning.

As we age, the window to learning how to communicate as a native speaker in a new language decreases. For those of us raised in the United States school system, it's common to begin learning how to understand and communicate in a second language in high school, which is not the optimal time for our brains to acquire it. By high school, the average American student's day is stuffed to the brim with English—unless, of course, they come from a bilingual or multilingual family. Academics and other life events typically take precedence over second language learning.[4]

When we're communicating with a toddler, we can tend to be more patient, speak in simple sentences, and repeat phrases and words for them to learn. As we age, those behaviors are not typical for adults speaking with other adults or adolescents. We're already focused on teaching them language because we're teaching them to "talk." This is the perfect opportunity to reinforce one word at a time during daily routines. We can give them the same simple, single words in another language and repeat it to reinforce the memorization. For example, during breakfast, when they reach for their cup, you can say "cup" in both languages for them to hear the "word" for this item when they have it in their hands and want to use it. This makes them more motivated to pay attention to the learning opportunity because they are actively engaging with the item while you teach them the word or label it in one or two languages.

TERMS TO KNOW

Monolingual: This term refers to someone who speaks and understands only one language.

Bilingual: This term refers to someone who speaks and understands two languages.

Multilingual: This term refers to someone or something (books, resources, etc.) that speak/include more than one language.

There are many benefits of exposure to more than one language. Here are only a few examples:

1. Cognitive Development (The Way a Child's Brain Grows)
    - Promote creativity and can help slow down dementia as we age.[5] (It might seem odd to talk about dementia in a toddler book. However, all our brains age. If we could provide our children with a leg up in preventing cognitive decline later on, wouldn't we?)

- Create mental flexibility, enhance problem-solving skills, and improve attention management.[6]

TO LEARN MORE

There are so many amazing resources available about multilingual children. Here are a few:

- *Raising a Bilingual Child: A Step-by-Step Guide for Parents* by Barbara Zurer Pearson[7]
- "Bilingualism in Young Children: Separating Fact from Fiction" by Lauren Lowry Hanen[8]
- *Welcome to Your Child's Brain* by Sandra Aamodt and Sam Wang[9]
- The Multilingual Learning Toolkit[10]
- The Linguistic Society[11]
- *Promoting the Educational Success of Children and Youth Learning English: Promising Futures* from the National Academies of Sciences, Engineering, and Medicine[12]

The resources are cited at the end of this book.

2. Social Advantages
   - Increased ability to build relationships with people who speak a language other than English.
   - Increased cultural awareness. Families move because of different circumstances. Imagine your child gets a new classmate from a country that doesn't speak

English. It may sound silly to hear as an adult, but if a child has never been exposed to another language, they might not know that other languages exist at all! If a new classmate shows up without the ability to speak English, a child with some knowledge of other languages may be more welcoming rather than treating them differently.

- Develop empathy. It's hard to learn another language. In the above example, if the new classmate is frustrated or afraid in their environment, your child may be the one who treats them with kindness. Even if they don't realize why they feel an innate sense of understanding toward different languages, it will be instilled in them because you tried to learn together. Children look to their caregivers to learn how to react to all differences, whether that's someone whose language is unfamiliar or someone with different cultural beliefs.

GOOD NEWS!

If you are a practitioner working with the early intervention populations, do your research. If you overhear practitioners encouraging families to only speak one language at home or to their toddler, this is your opportunity to share great news with them and advocate for bilingual or multilingual educational opportunities. Denying a child these opportunities can not only isolate them from family engagement but also deprive them of additional cognitive, social, and academic opportunities only available to bilingual or multilingual children. It is easier to ask a family to speak only the language you speak as a professional coming into their home or teaching the child. However, we can spread good news and advocate for toddlers who cannot yet advocate for themselves.

How to Expose Your Monolingual Child to Another Language

So you'd love to expose your child to a second language, but you failed high school Spanish. Don't worry! There are different ways to bring another language or languages into your child's life. (Keep in mind that this is not an exhaustive list.)

Here are a few examples:

1. Language immersion programs

These are programs that provide a child with an opportunity to learn a second language from teachers/staff who speak that language fluently in an academic atmosphere. The earlier the exposure, the better! Sometimes, these are part-time programs during the day, weekends, or after school hours. Ask around for language immersion programs in your area by talking to local school districts, places of worship, and babysitting boards. Using these resources, I discovered a program in my area that starts a child at six weeks old and two programs that continue into elementary age.

2. Access to native speakers, such as those at a local church, diverse community center, or au pair or bilingual babysitter

Most of us need some degree of childcare. My husband and I both work full-time jobs and enjoy our careers. Since we need childcare, why not make the most of it? Choosing a bilingual babysitter or toddler language immersion class, setting your monolingual babysitter/classroom up with audio and physical books in other languages, or recommending teaching songs and social games in other languages creates learning opportunities by optimizing their time spent away from you as a potentially meaningful language learning experience that may set them up for success in the future.

3. Audiobooks and songs

Many of the books you already read with your child are available in bilingual versions. They will already know the story, and you will be able to point out the translated text and practice together. Listening to the audio versions of the book recorded by a native speaker will help with pronunciation, intonation, and the nuances of that second language. You can also watch videos of native speakers reading the books and turn the pages together. It can be a fun bonding experience for you and your child to learn a second language together.

Children with Disabilities and Bilingualism

Even if your child has a developmental disability, they can still be provided with the opportunity to learn a second language without detriment to their development.[13] I have worked with many families who speak Spanish as their primary language and have a child or children with a disability, and they reported being told by providers to stop speaking Spanish to their children because of "bilingualism confusing children." There is no negative impact for a child with a disability to be raised in a bilingual environment.[14] In fact, alienating a child by refusing to teach them the language primarily spoken in the home deprives them of language learning opportunities and building relationships with family members. When a child has a disability such as a speech and language disorder, autism, or developmental disorder, they are in need of language learning opportunities to learn how to adequately communicate their needs and wants, advocate for themselves, build relationships, and so on. To gain essential communication skills and build relationships with family members, the child may need to be bilingual.

Advocate for families around you. If you hear people say they are unable to speak their native language to their child, encourage them to conduct their own research and do what would be most beneficial for their child and family.

No two children, families, or family situations are exactly the same. All families and children are unique with their own unique needs and goals. These are suggestions. I always urge my families to do their own research and do what works best for their individual family. If you're given a recommendation by a provider and feel it is not right, such as only speaking one language to your child, advocate for what you think is best.

In the next chapter, we'll get into a subject that affects many of my patients and their families: concerning behaviors.

CHAPTER 3

CONCERNING BEHAVIORS

DISCLAIMER

The goal of this chapter is for a caregiver to understand that if their kiddo is throwing the occasional tantrum, the issue might be rooted in a communication breakdown. But it is in no way meant to be an exhaustive resource on concerning behaviors, especially those that disrupt daily life. There are numerous resources available that appropriately address concerns such as head banging, drawing blood, or excessive or consistent hairpulling. I recommend seeking professional guidance at that point. One approach I recommend for severe concerning behaviors is functional communication training.[1]

Raise your hand if your child has thrown a tantrum to communicate.

You're not alone. My hand is *way* up in the air!

It's called the "terrible twos" for a reason, but if that's how you label that year of your child's life, it is sure to be a "terrible" year!

What if we looked at these years differently? What if we looked at these pivotal years in our children's development as opportunities to teach them the language and social skills they will need to be successful in advocating for themselves, building meaningful relationships, and beginning a rewarding academic career? Without changing who our children are or dimming their fun and spunky personalities, we can provide them with opportunities to learn more complex and safer communication skills.

Around two years of age, children often experience a language explosion.[2] I've heard parents say that overnight, their child started speaking in full sentences. This may not be entirely true, but it can certainly feel that way! All of a sudden, a child's vocabulary and language use seem to go from a handful of words to fifty words. This is a great time to teach your child that their words are powerful and that the concerning behaviors they may default to are not as effective at getting their needs met as using a gesture, word, or phrase.

You can do this by teaching them to communicate their needs in a safer manner. We're replacing the concerning behavior with a gesture, word, or phrase[3] that they can use easily. This decreases the concerning behaviors and increases calm words, gestures, and potentially visuals (if they need this). We're setting them (and ourselves) up for more positive relationships, emotional support, and a potentially more positive outlook on life.

In this chapter you will gain an understanding of how important communication is, especially during the toddler years, and how the concerning behaviors that may trouble you could be your child's primary way of communicating. We'll discuss how to identify a concerning behavior as communication and how to give your child the tools they need to communicate.

What Is a Concerning Behavior?

Concerning behaviors are tantrums, throwing, kicking, hitting, or any action that could potentially be dangerous for the child or others around them. These behaviors can occur at any age. However, we usually begin to see them in the toddler years as children learn to communicate, regulate emotions, and navigate life as a small human.

Let's look at a real-life example of a concerning behavior and how we addressed it.

Ben was a two-year-old who primarily used gestures and spoke at the one-word level to communicate with people he knew well. I consulted with Ben and his family while he was waiting for his speech and language services to begin and for a few sessions afterward.

Normally, his mother anticipated his needs and would provide him with snacks and regular mealtimes at home. At day care he ate at scheduled times. However, when he was hungry or thirsty outside of these times, he would throw his cup and screamed. If he was not immediately given the snack or juice he wanted, he would escalate his tantrum by falling on the floor. These tantrums began to become a regular occurrence with Ben.

These scenarios would play out several times a week and began to decrease when we got to the core of the concerning behaviors, which meant teaching Ben to communicate what he needed *before* the throwing began. Instead of putting all the snacks/drinks/toys that he might want in front of him, we started creating opportunities for Ben to practice asking for them.

When we saw that his cup was empty, we had juice and water close by and taught Ben how to advocate for himself in a safer way by using the words "juice" or "water." His family began practicing this and teaching him to verbally communicate his requests for snacks, food, drinks, and people instead of automatically giving him what they thought he might want. After only one session, Ben was able to request his "juice." With the consistency of teaching him to communicate at home, Ben no longer needed to use concerning behaviors to get his needs met; he was consistently using words and gestures instead. In the moments when Ben would revert to his concerning behaviors to communicate. His family would use the same series of strategies, such as finding out what Ben was trying to communicate (i.e., wanting food because of hunger) and teaching him another way to communicate this need in a safer way.

WHEN CONCERNING BEHAVIORS AFFECT YOUR DAILY LIFE

I want to preface this chapter by saying that if your child has severe concerning behaviors that are affecting your family life on a daily basis, you should use more than this book as a resource. Some of the more severe concerning behaviors include head banging, any self-injurious behavior, or behavior that injures someone around them mentally or physically. This isn't the time to wait. This is the time to get support in place for your child and your family immediately.

Intensive intervention may be warranted. When a two-year-old is using a concerning behavior that's hurting them or someone else, you may not consider it a big deal. But if the behavior hasn't changed by the time they're ten years old, you'll be in a different spot in regard to potential injuries. I have been consulted on many occasions regarding preschool and elementary children to address concerning behaviors that, according to their parents, started in the toddler years. Early intervention is the key to successfully learning safer behaviors and gaining family support.

Reach out to your child's pediatrician and speak to them about services for you and your child. You can find a board-certified behavior analyst (BA) for your child at the Behavior Analyst Certification Board at www.bacb.com. Your insurance provider can be a resource in letting you know what behavior services they cover, as well as how much and where they will cover the services. Advocate for parent coaching to be provided on the strategies the BA is using, as well as for *any* educational or medical services your child (and you!) are receiving. If you are not comfortable with an intervention/strategy/person during services, tell them to stop using the strategy and provide you with alternatives that fit your comfort level and family values and culture.

Communication

Expressive and Receptive Language

Being proactive in teaching communication skills and using the strategies in this book may help decrease concerning behaviors your child uses to communicate.

First, let's dive into what "communication" is. Communication occurs when there is a speaker and a listener. A speaker uses gestures, vocal speech, or visuals to send a message to another person, which is then received by a listener. The listener uses their senses, such as sight, hearing, and sometimes touch to receive that message. Effective communication[4] is imperative to allow a person to get their needs met, establish relationships, advocate for themselves, and express emotions.

The speaker uses "expressive" language. The inability to share wants, needs, thoughts, feelings, and so on could be labeled as an expressive language disorder.[5] The listener uses "receptive" language because they receive the message.

This may all seem obvious, but it's important to understand the foundation of communication to help your child increase the effectiveness of their speech and language skills. I'm going to use the terms expressive and receptive language when referring to communication skills throughout this book.

The Roots of Concerning Behaviors Related to Communication Skills

Here are a few reasons why a concerning communication behavior might occur:

1. When our kiddos use the concerning behavior that successfully meets a specific need, they essentially learn to use it again. The concerning behavior may not have worked with you, but someone in our child's life taught them this behavior works to communicate their specific need. Of course, they'll try it again with us and others in their life to see if the desired result continues to happen.

TO LEARN MORE

To learn more about "challenging (concerning) behaviors as communication" from the Evidence-Based Instructional Practices,[6] refer to the fully cited resource at the end of this book.

For example, Ben wanted something to drink, so he threw his empty sippy cup. Grandma looks at his empty cup on the floor and says, "Oh, it's empty! Let me get you more juice." Ben learned that he could throw his empty cup when he wanted more juice, which resulted in an adult getting him more juice.

2. They are unable to use another communication skill, and the concerning behavior is all they have to use to communicate this specific need. It may be because they have not learned how to use a specific word or gesture, or they might be using what they think is the correct word/gesture/phrase but are not understood. Their language skills may not have yet caught up to what they are being asked to do.

For example, Ethan, a three-year-old, communicates using single words/sounds and gestures. He has a speech and language disorder and is trying to put his shoes on to go outside and play. He is having trouble putting his shoes on and gets frustrated because they do not fit properly. He starts crying and walks over to his dad with one of his shoes. He is working on learning to expressively say the word "help" but is currently unable to use it naturally throughout the day. His father sees him crying with his shoe and helps him put it on properly. In this scenario Ethan does not yet have the word "help" or the gesture of "giving his shoes" to his dad to communicate that he needs help. Crying is the only way he can communicate at that moment.

When our kiddos are sick, not feeling well, or have not slept or eaten well, they may not be able to use new or complex words/phrases/gestures. During these times they may use concerning behaviors to communicate their needs even if they generally communicate at a more complex level. Have patience during these moments and model the words or gestures you want to teach them to use when they are in a better space for learning. Write down the words, gestures, or phrases you may want to take time teaching when they are back to feeling like themselves (or close to themselves).

How Can I Turn a Communicative Behavior of Concern into a Safer Behavior?

As caregivers we need to have realistic expectations for our kiddos. Sometimes, we may hope they will or expect them to use a new word, phrase, or gesture, but it may be too hard for them based on their current skills and strengths. It could also simply be the wrong moment for a learning opportunity because of a number of reasons we've already discussed. If they're upset because they've been ill for two days, that's not a great teaching moment for you to insist that they learn to say "My stomach hurts."

However, if your child is feeling fine and it's an ideal time for language learning, we can teach them a safer way to communicate rather than throwing a tantrum or kicking, biting, crying, and so on.

To do this, take an inventory of your child's strengths. You can use the following chart to help:

COMPLETED CHART EXAMPLE: SAM, TWENTY-FOUR MONTHS	
Current Communication Skills: Spend five minutes, three times a day, for three days with the goal of observing and listening to your child. Watch your child as they play, eat, read books, and interact with you and others around them. Keep this chart with you, and write down the gestures they use, the sounds (both vowels and consonant sounds) you hear, and the words and phrases they say. Remember, these words and phrases do not need to be perfect. If you know what word they are using, then note the way they are saying it, as well as the word they are trying to say.	
Gestures my child is using	*Use the gestures list from the first chapter to help you complete this list.* Pointing, giving, reaching, smiling, eye contact, kisses
Sounds my child is using	*Keep in mind the developmentally appropriate sounds mentioned in chapter 1.* B, D, K, G, O, U, I, W, M, N, E, P, A
Words my child is using	*These can be emotion words such as "wee" and "oh no," as well as sounds such as animal sounds—"moo" for a cow, "quack" for a duck, or "vroom" for a car.* "Ep" (help), "ini" (mimi), mom, pop, wee, go, "id" (outside), peppa

COMPLETED CHART EXAMPLE: SAM, TWENTY-FOUR MONTHS *continued*	
Phrases my child is using	I wanna go I go No, ep (No, help) Go id (Go outside)

TO LEARN MORE

To learn more about the idea behind capturing a sample of your child's language, look at the resource "Language Sample Collection and Analysis" from the *Journal of Speech, Language, and Hearing Research*. The goal is for you to pay attention to the language your child is using on a daily basis.[7]

CHART TO COMPLETE
Current Communication Skills: Spend five minutes, three times a day, for three days with the goal of observing and listening to your child. Watch your child as they play, eat, read books, and interact with you and others around them. Keep this chart with you, and write down the gestures they use, the sounds (both vowels and consonant sounds) you hear, and the words and phrases they say. Remember, these words and phrases do not need to be perfect. If you know what word they are using, then note the way they are saying it, as well as the word they are trying to say.

CHART TO COMPLETE *continued*	
Gestures my child is using	*Use the gestures list from the first chapter to help you complete this list.*
Sounds my child is using	*Keep in mind the developmentally appropriate sounds mentioned in chapter 1.*
Words my child is using	*These can be emotion words such as "wee" and "oh no," as well as sounds such as animal sounds—"moo" for a cow, "quack" for a duck, or "vroom" for a car.*
Phrases my child is using	

Use the above chart to choose which communication skill (gesture/word/phrase) you will teach your child to use to communicate instead of the concerning behavior. The goal is to teach to their strengths and use another way (gestural, visual, or verbal) to communicate that same need. When they use a concerning behavior to communicate a specific need, we want to teach them a quick and easy, safer communication skill to use. By looking at the current communication skills they use on a daily basis using the chart above, you will have quick access to an inventory of their skills. Create opportunities for your child to practice using this safer communication skill.

TEACH TO THEIR STRENGTHS		
Concerning behavior (Insert the concerning behavior here, along with why you think that behavior is happening, in as much detail as you feel is appropriate.)	**Communication skill I will teach (to replace the concerning behavior)** (Write down a communication skill from the first chart here that you will teach your child to use instead.)	**Person(s) to help** (Write people's names down here who will help teach your child. *Consistency is key.* This could be babysitters, grandparents, nannies, au pairs, day care teachers, older siblings, or anyone who will be around your child.)
*Sam is sitting on the floor **kicking the door** when he **wants to go outside**.*	*He is able to say "Go id" (Go outside) and point to what he wants. I'm going to teach him to point to the door and say, "Go id." When I model the words (say the words to him to teach this new skill), I will say the full words, "Go outside," to give him the correct full word that he can learn to use over time.*	*When his babysitter is watching him this week, I will tell her to refrain from opening the door to let Sam play outside when he is kicking the door and teach him to say "Go outside," while pointing to the door. Immediately, we will open the door for him to go play, teaching him the new more complex communication skill of saying "Go outside" in place of kicking.*

TEACH TO THEIR STRENGTHS *continued*		
Sam is ***throwing himself*** *on the couch and whining* ***when he wants*** *to watch* Peppa Pig *in the living room.*	*He is able to say "Peppa" and point, so when Sam throws himself on the couch and whines, I will teach him to tell me he wants to watch* Peppa Pig *by pointing to the TV and saying, "Peppa."*	*When his dad is watching him on Saturday, I will encourage him to teach Sam to use the new communication skill so that he, too, can see a decrease in Sam throwing himself on the couch in the living room.*

Goal Shifting to Receptive Language

When I help caregivers work through concerning behaviors, one of the first questions they ask is what to do when their child clearly communicates a desire that is off-limits, such as wanting TV time or going outside when it's bedtime. How can I simultaneously praise them for communicating while also saying no to their request?

The answer is shifting to receptive language. Our goal is still communication, just receptive language instead (i.e., following a direction to go to bed), not expressive language (i.e., using a new sentence). You can praise them for using a new word or communicating nicely, but that does not serve as an alternative to going to bed.

Imagine you've just gotten your two-year-old ready for bed, and she looks at you with a big smile and says, "Outside" or "I want to go outside!" This is especially notable considering that just a few weeks ago, she used to stand at the door screaming when she wanted to go outside and would have a complete meltdown if she couldn't. (You might feel somewhat timid to say no, even if there's an active thunderstorm!)

You're floored that she spoke in a full sentence and that she's managing her emotions. However, you can't always honor a request, even if your child has made vast improvements.

Basically, we're going to tell them, "Wow! Nice job telling me you want to go outside. I can't wait to go outside with you tomorrow. Right now, it's bedtime."

One strategy is to make the alternate activities more fun. In the Daily Routines and Strategies part of this book, there's a section for "My child doesn't want to do this activity" or "What happens if my child doesn't like this?" This can be a good resource to make these times more fun.

So in the above example for the little girl who wanted to go outside at bedtime, the caregiver could say, "Wow, I really love how you said that! I love being outside, too! But right now it's nighttime, and we have to go to bed. So let's go put [child's favorite stuffed animal] to bed. He's so tired right now. Let's tuck him in together."

You could give them two choices, such as "Do you want to skip to your bed? Or do you want to crawl like a spider?"

Expressive Language Strategies

When your goal is expressive language, such as communicating using more complex language, here are a few tips to keep in mind:

1. Capitalize on in-the-moment learning opportunities.

When your child uses a concerning behavior to communicate, immediately teach them to use a safer communication skill that is easy for them, such as pointing at a visual cue (more on that later). Try not to give in, if you're able to, and use that moment as a quick opportunity to teach them that a safer communication skill will be effective in communicating their needs. Model the communication skill you know they can use instead. Immediately after they follow your model, give them the activity/person/thing they wanted to reinforce the skill.

If your child is screaming, "Mom!" to get your attention because their show just ended but you want them to say "Mom" in a calm way, then you can model saying, "Mom," in a calm voice for them, ideally up to two times. Model it once (making sure you have their attention—get on their level and make eye contact) and say, "Mom," in the calm tone you'd like to hear them adopt. Count in your head up to five. If you don't hear them say "Mom" calmly, model it again. Now if they do say "Mom" calmly, praise them for that and meet their need immediately after by putting on another episode of the show or whatever they were requesting.

If they don't follow your lead, we will still model by calmly saying, "Mom," and getting their need met by using a gesture instead, such as handing you the remote. If they don't follow the model, we want to be neutral. Still meet their need(s). If needed, find something else you can positively comment on, for example, maybe their body is calm. So you say, "Oh, your body is so calm. Let me change the channel for you." That way we're at least getting feedback that calm is what gets their need met.

Write this scenario down and provide learning opportunities throughout the day that are less than a minute long of learning how to get your attention using a calm voice.

Teach others around them to use immediate feedback as

well. The quicker they receive consistent exposure to learning how to use safer/more complex communication skills, the quicker our kiddos will learn to stop using the concerning behavior.

2. Meet the child where they are.

If you see your child use a facial grimace or begin to become frustrated when you are modeling the new gesture/word/phrase for them, assume that they are unable to use the new skill at that moment. Instead of pushing them past their limits, choose an easier communication skill, such as a simple gesture (pointing, tapping, giving, looking in the direction of the item/person they want) or just looking at you and listening to you model the new word/phrase/gesture. The goal is not for our children to become frustrated or upset; rather, it is the exact opposite: we want to teach them *not* to resort to a concerning behavior but to use the communication skills they use at other times during the day.

Building off the example above, if your child screams, "Mom!" to get your attention, the example isn't to model "Mom, I really need your help right now to use the remote to put on a new episode of my show that just ended." The child is only using one word at a time. Always keep your child's communication level and style in mind and meet them there. We aren't trying to build on their language when our goal is to replace a concerning behavior; we're simply matching it or making it easier. If your child didn't say "Mom" calmly, note that we mentioned teaching them to use an easier skill, such as calmly handing over the remote, or giving them positive feedback on their calm body language, and then meeting their need.

3. Honor and recognize their progress.

For example, if your son is hitting you to get your attention and you've been working on getting him to gently tap you instead, you need to praise him when he taps you. "Wow, you tapped me! I love how you did that. Yes, my little love, what do you need?" Reward him with immediate attention and praise them specifically for using their new skill. If we're teaching the skill but not honoring it when they use it, they will resort back to the other behavior, such as hitting, because that *always* gets attention.

Building on Your Child's Strengths

I was working with a two-year-old named Alex who was nonverbal. He did not enjoy physical closeness. He rejected touch and didn't like when strangers got close to him. His mother was frustrated. "I just want him to tell me what he needs," she told me. (By the way, if you've had that thought or feeling, just know that you aren't alone. Many of the parents I've worked with have said the same thing.)

Alex's mom was meeting all his physical needs as far as keeping him well fed, entertained, and well rested. She also took him to an occupational therapist, feeding therapist, and speech therapist (me).

As much as I understood his mom's desire to have Alex say her name or give her a big hug, we simply weren't going to get there without taking many, many baby steps on the way. First, I had to identify Alex's strengths while getting him to feel comfortable with me.

His mom told me that Alex loved bubbles, which was helpful intel. I had a tube of bubbles in my bag. I sat on the floor across from Alex and blew a big stream of bubbles into the air. This got his attention. Then I recapped the bubbles and rolled the tube across the floor to him. He responded by rolling the tube in a similar manner. I blew another stream, which he enjoyed. I rolled the tube back to him. He rolled it back to me. Repeat.

Soon, Alex learned that I would blow the bubbles if he simply touched the tube. By the end of a thirty-minute session, Alex stood up, carried the tube, and handed it to me. His mother cried. She'd never seen him do something like this before.

Over the next several sessions, Alex handed me a cup, a diaper, or an empty snack container to ask for something. He was recognizing the function of these real objects and using the "give" gestures (which is handing or potentially pointing) to communicate a need. We created a board where some items he commonly needed could be easily found.

Alex had success in communicating because we built on his existing skills. We found that he liked bubbles, then built slowly upon that.

If there's anything I want you to learn from Alex's story, it's that you can't expect your child to go from point A to point D or E. Recognizing their existing skills and building onto those is generally the best way forward.

The Importance of Emotional Literacy

Toddlers have many big emotions. Emotional literacy gives the opportunity for kiddos to express what they're experiencing in a safer way. Learning not just how to control them but also what they mean helps them learn more complex language and helps caregivers know how best to support them.

Emotional literacy is the ability to verbalize your emotions and understand the words and labels that pertain to certain emotions in a developmentally appropriate way.

It's helpful for children to learn that other people have emotions as well. They aren't using a deep theory of mind understanding but being able to recognize that other people have similar feelings as well. Even the dog can be helpful to teach emotional literacy—"Look, Spot is excited, isn't she?"

This is the very beginning of empathy. At this age they think that their mom is the only mom in the world. They think the day starts when they wake up, and the day ends when they go to bed.

How to Teach Emotional Literacy

TO LEARN MORE

To learn more about teaching emotional literacy, I recommend the "Pyramid Model" resource from the Center on the Social and Emotional Foundations for Early Learning at Vanderbilt University.[8]

There's an interesting intersection between emotional literacy and language learning. It's one thing to feel an emotion and identify it and another to know the word and say it aloud. (I know many adults who can't identify their own emotions, even if they know the words!) It's way more challenging to be a child and not have the ability to recognize *or* name these big emotions. Sometimes, concerning behaviors arise out of this space, which can be hard to navigate, whether or not your child is consistently using clear verbal communication. Here are some ways we can teach emotional literacy *and* help our kids learn the appropriate words:

1. Modeling

The adult models experiencing an emotion and naming it in a scenario. While smiling, the adult says, "I'm so happy to see you!" or "I'm sad it's raining and we can't play outside, too."

2. Naming an emotion for them

The child is playing with a peer, and one takes the other's toy. His shoulders are slumped over, his head is down, and he has tears in his eyes, which are clear signs of sadness. You might say, "Wow, it looks like that made you sad." That gives them a word that they can use next time they feel that way.

You have to be sure to use the correct word for what they appear to be experiencing, even if it isn't what you want them to feel. If your toddler hits you and is laughing, you wouldn't say, "Hitting makes me sad." Instead, you might put the emotional learning opportunity onto yourself. "I'm feeling hurt because I don't want to be hit. We are going to have to do something different now." Or "You can hit a pillow if you're frustrated but not mommy."

3. Reading books

Books are an opportunity to take yourself out of a scenario and watch a character experience these words you've been feeling. I enjoy using the Daniel Tiger books for this purpose. In one book Daniel is really sad. If we're playing with something at the end of their session and the kiddo is sad that we have to stop playing with the toy, we can map that onto what Daniel Tiger was feeling in the book we just read.

4. Creating an emotional check-in section of the house

This is a place where you've taped pictures of faces experiencing different emotions onto the wall or perhaps put them in a little notebook they can flip through. This can be any corner of any room, as long as it's fairly quiet and can be used consistently for this purpose. Outside the pictures of emotions, you could add some other comforting activities to help the child wind down. I've worked with some kiddos who just want to face plant into a large pillow and need to stay that way for a few seconds when they're having a big emotion. I had another who loved water, so we made a shallow container of water so she could run her fingers through it as a way to calm down. This place isn't only for when they're feeling upset. It can also be a safe spot to jump up and down when excited. This should not feel like time-out. I've seen many children learn to use these corners independently when they're feeling strong emotions.

RESOURCES: NATIONAL CENTER FOR PYRAMID MODEL INNOVATIONS

Here are some of my favorite books for teaching emotions to young children. Check out the Book Nook from the National Center for Pyramid Model Innovations[9] for all their recommended books by age.

Focus on teaching your child one emotion for a week or two (depending on your child's age, developmental skills, and your family time).

- *Glad Monster, Sad Monster*
- *Llama Llama Misses Mama*
- *Alphabreaths*
- *Guess How Much I love You*
- *The Rainbow Fish*
- *Too Loud Lily*

Resource Share: The National Center for Pyramid Model Innovations has several books, printouts, and activities designed for caregivers and teachers to use to teach social emotional skills. I have used these resources for many years and walked caregivers through their social-emotional programs and have respect for the research conducted by the creators and development team behind these programs.

Throughout part 2, keep in mind that these behaviors may stem from the fact that the child can't make the sound or gestures you're modeling, or they simply might not want to. Illness, lack of sleep, and so on are also factors in behaviors. Be sure to be aware of these types of factors and modify your goals with these in mind.

In the next chapter, we'll discuss how to make the most out of your sessions with an SLP so both you and your child will feel empowered by the sessions.

CHAPTER 4

MAKING THE MOST OF SPEECH AND LANGUAGE SESSIONS

Daily life is busy, and we're all trying to navigate it the best way we can. On top of all other appointments and life demands, parents or caregivers with children receiving additional services, such as speech and language, now need to drive to a speech and language clinic for a thirty-minute to an hour-long session once a week (or more) and then drive home or back to day care. Sometimes parents have to take time off work for these sessions. Believe me, I understand it's a lot!

If you're making it work, you will thank yourself later when your child is making progress (assuming they are receiving high-quality services) and learning the skills they need to be successful academically and socially for the rest of their lives. The sooner your child receives high-quality services, the better.

But even the highest-quality speech-language pathologist (SLP) is probably only face-to-face with your child a few hours per week. It's important to continue to reinforce the lessons your child learned in their speech and language sessions even when they're at home. I encourage you to be in the sessions as much as possible. A thirty-minute session to an hour a week is nothing compared with the time you spend with them during meals, dressing routines, and other morning and daily routines. For this reason, this book is designed to incorporate language learning opportunities into the routines you are already doing with your child on a daily (or almost daily) basis. Life is busy, and this is one shortcut we can use to save time while setting our children up for success.

In this chapter I will teach you how to get the most out of your child's speech and language sessions by continually building your relationship with your child's SLP and creating opportunities during the day to practice your child's speech and language goals outside the sessions, as well as opportunities to advocate for what you believe is best for your child and your family.

What Is Speech and Language Therapy?

Speech and language therapy during the toddler years helps support a child's speech, language, feeding, and social communication skills. It may be surprising to learn that we can help with feeding and mealtime routines, as well as with speech! We may assess the movement and control involved with eating. The mouth and tongue affect far more than just speech.

The speech-language pathologist, or SLP, is a professional who gives speech and language therapy sessions. An SLP is someone who has spent their graduate and possibly their undergraduate work in studying communication disorders, typical communication, swallowing, and related services across the lifespan. An SLP with a certificate of clinical competence has spent an additional year beyond graduate school specializing in the field and maintaining their certification through the American Speech-Language-Hearing Association (ASHA).

Here are a few quick points on different skills an SLP may work on with your child. (Check in regularly with your child's SLP for goal updates.)

1. Speech

These are the sounds that come out of the mouth and the way they are produced. We use our "articulators" (tongue, cheeks, teeth, lips, and nose) to produce individual sounds, words, and sentences. This is your intonation, loudness, and unique qualities that make your individual voice. Sometimes, these sounds can be distorted, which produces a different sound from the one attempted or results in the omission of the sound. An example of this in a toddler-age child would be saying "kog" instead of "dog" or "unny" instead of "bunny" because they have distorted or omitted the initial consonant sound. Additionally, an articulator may not move where/how it should to make a particular sound, such as when the lips come together to make a "b" sound. If the lips don't come together, it just sounds like "uhh." Some toddlers may make the sound in the back of their mouth, resulting in a different sound, such as saying "goo" instead of "boo." An SLP can identify where and how an individual sound is produced and the differences behind the difficulty in producing a certain sound. They can create exercises and activities to help your toddler produce their desired sound or new sound to increase their speech intelligibility (the amount of their sounds and words that are understood by others).

2. Language

These are the words that we string together to form phrases and sentences. Toddlers are learning how to put words together, where to use them, and how to change them to communicate a specific message. For example, suppose a child is trying to get your attention using a single word such as "Hungry" to communicate that they're hungry. In that case, an SLP can help build on their existing skills to teach them about different types of food and snacks so they can specifically communicate their needs, such as learning to say the specific food item they are hungry for or how to ask for it. Language is the structure of the words we are stringing together, the meaning of words, and grammar.

3. Feeding

These are mealtime strategies, such as how to safely swallow and eat new foods, as well as mealtime skills needed to successfully consume calories. Sometimes, aversion to foods doesn't simply boil down to pickiness. It could stem from a food allergy or that our child has a sensory (visual, textural, or smell) experience different from ours with a particular food or setting that we're working through. For example, if a child is only eating bland solid foods such as goldfish or white bread, then we would try to determine the root cause and expand their food repertoire. By teaching them to safely consume fruits, vegetables, and a wider variety of foods, we can expand their mealtime food opportunities based on a family's culture and the medical and behavioral differences present in the child.

4. Social Communication

This is how we use language to send and receive messages. For toddlers, this means learning how to use speech and language to build relationships, express emotions, send messages, and understand the components of communication (receptive and expressive). Some kiddos with differences in their language development might get frustrated instead of identifying what they need help with and finding a person to ask for help. If the child is only using vowel sounds and gestures to communicate, an SLP might teach them how to ask for help in other ways, such as walking to their caregiver and providing them with the item they need help with, making eye contact with them, and maybe even saying, "Help." The point is finding a person and sending that message to them instead of becoming frustrated without realizing the next step in making their communication skills more complex.

TO LEARN MORE

To learn more about the professional track or the profession of speech-language pathology, the American Speech-Language-Hearing Association (ASHA) is a great resource. ASHA is the governing body for the profession in the United States. Visit www.asha.org.

You can also learn more about speech and language sessions and find an ASHA-certified speech-language pathologist who specializes in the topic and age group you have questions about on the ASHA website. For caregivers whose children are already receiving speech therapy, the website can also help you understand the specific therapy your child is receiving.

Be in the Know

Communicate regularly with your child's SLP, especially during the toddler years, which are pivotal in setting the stage for their academic and social lives. After the toddler years, if your child attends therapy with an SLP, you may be much less involved on a session-by-session basis. (Even if you are available, you may not be able to view all sessions because they are being held with other children during the school day.) The treating SLP will be focused on academics and communication as opposed to focusing on family goals. Communicating your child's progress on goals with you and how to carry over working on these at home varies from SLP to SLP and school to school. But during the toddler years, parents and caregivers have the opportunity to be fully involved in goal-making, as these goals are designed with the family in mind, not solely academics, and in watching the sessions. Caregivers can also make a great impact in their child's language at home. You want to know what your child is practicing and the rationale (or why) behind the strategies that the treating SLP is using. Here are a few ways you can do this:

1. Attend all the sessions you can.

I recommend attending all your child's sessions during the toddler years, even if you are out of sight—whether observing live or remote, using Zoom (or another secure video conferencing platform), or watching a recording of the session. This will allow you to see firsthand which strategies are being used and how your child is progressing. As a practitioner, I have recorded many sessions and set up a Zoom video conference during sessions when parents needed to work or could not attend live. You don't need to watch the whole session, just one or two activities. (I have recorded the whole session or a few activities, depending on the needs of the child and parent requests so caregivers could watch what they chose to watch.) Build a plan for your child's SLP so that you can stay up to date on goals and strategies you can use at home to supplement their services.

2. Ask for data.

Ask the SLP to show you the growth in your child's skills, which may include how many times your child used their target gesture, sound, word, or phrase, and share your home data with the SLP. This could be the same gesture, sound, word, or phrase they are practicing at home or a communication skill you have seen at home that you're teaching your child to use instead of a concerning behavior.

3. Create a notebook.

If you're unable to attend your child's sessions (remotely or live), create a notebook for your child's SLP to take notes in each session and use to communicate with you. You and the SLP can pass it back and forth to communicate the skills your child is building, ask and answer questions, and track their progress.

4. Create a meaningful way for YOU to practice new skills with your child.

Describe a routine that goes well at home, and work with the SLP to create opportunities to teach one skill at home before your child's next therapy session. This will help increase your child's learning opportunities and consistency in using their new skills. A single weekly session can be helpful but not as much as several five-minute sessions several times per day or week. Aim for a total of thirty minutes a day, dispersed among the things you're already doing—the premise of this book!

5. Use the strategies in part 2 by incorporating your child's personalized speech and language goals into the activities.

It can take less than five minutes to view an activity that your child is doing with their SLP and think about next steps or write down a question in the notebook you share with their SLP. You can use this chart as a jumping-off point.

Note: Some of these questions may not apply to your specific child, so add or change the questions to fit your family and child's needs.

SLP SESSION LEARNING	
Questions to Ask	**Write Answers Here**
I see you used (insert strategy/activity/item/ person) in my child's session. Why was that used?	
I saw my child was able to use (insert sound/word/ phrase/gesture) for the first time. How did you get him to use that new communication skill?	
Describe one activity I can use this week to help my child work on a goal from the session today.	
What is one new gesture/ sound/word/phrase/skill my child learned today?	
Other	

Advocating for Evidenced-Based Practices and Modes of Communication/ Languages Represented in Your Home

As with all highly individualized therapies, one size does *not* fit all in speech-language pathology. Moreover, the field is constantly advancing, meaning strategies that were once considered the norm get replaced by more updated ones.

There are many well-meaning people with "good" ideas or people who have been in the speech and language field for many years and "do what they have always done" with each child. Just as we, as adults, seek out and interview (if able) our medical team, change providers, and get second opinions (if able), treat your child's care in the same way.

Ask the SLP to provide you with a list of evidence-based practices they use in their sessions. In my initial assessment reports, I include evidenced-based practices I may use in my initial sessions and update them throughout the duration of treatment. I provide this to each family so they can explore the practices on their own or ask me questions.

Practitioners encounter new research on a daily basis. It is our duty to read it and apply it (if necessary) to our intervention approaches. As modern practices develop and society changes, we should adapt our therapeutic strategies accordingly. For example, an approach used for many years in speech and language sessions could consist of a child sitting at a table, working on flashcards or other activities while restricted to a table and high chair. This often meant struggling to keep the child's attention or to keep them sitting at the table, which took valuable time away from learning and teaching opportunities. A modern approach is more naturalistic. We get on the floor with the kiddos. We use snack times, outside play, daily routines, and games as learning opportunities, and we curl up in comfy chairs for preliteracy activities and language learning during book routines in a comfortable setting. But as is true with all science fields, we are always striving to find better evidence-based practices and apply them appropriately with the right child. As mentioned above, every child is different—some enjoy sitting in their high chair at the table for thirty minutes to engage in activities. Each child and their goals are taken into account, and therapeutic techniques should be designed around the unique child and teaching moments.

TO LEARN MORE

To learn more about a naturalistic approach, I recommend the "Naturalistic Intervention" module from the National Professional Development Center on Autism Spectrum Disorders.[1]

If your child has a particular diagnosis, such as autism or others, advocate for evidenced-based practices specifically tailored to your child and their diagnosis. The SLP serving your child should be able to share how they are using the evidenced-based practices. Learning these practices from the SLP can help you understand how to use them at home, in day care, and in other settings your child is in, creating consistency and increased high-quality learning opportunities throughout their day.

Visual Support Cues

I met Simon when he was almost three. At this time he was about to age out of my services. (I only served children up to age three at the time. He would be moving on to receive services through school, not through early intervention. This age differs from state to state.) His former services had been working with ASL communications with him, but gestural imitation was hard for him because of his language learning differences, and he had made little to no progress. He had received an autism diagnosis before he came to see me. His family reported he exhibited concerning behaviors all the time. He struggled to get his needs met because he relied solely on these concerning behaviors instead of using more complex, safer communication that his caregivers could understand.

For Simon's treatment plan, we started with basic communication. I found a toy that had a cause-and-effect feature; in this case, a spin top. I spun it, and when it stopped, he picked it up. My job is to find out what I can build off of what he's giving me, so I paused and waited for him to look at me. When he did, I saw that he wasn't holding the top, so I made it spin again, which he liked. This created a communication foundation for us and helped Simon understand that language learning would be fun. This created a relationship around language and play. This is an important foundation upon which to increase the complexity of their communication skills.

In the same session, we went from there to mealtime. Simon was in the habit of throwing anything he didn't want off his high chair and onto the floor. His mother was frustrated for wasting so much food, and Simon was also getting frustrated. We tried to figure out his favorite things, so I asked his mom what he ate regularly, and we printed out pictures of these foods. When he would touch a picture of it, we would give it to him. Within a month, he learned how to navigate a book of pictures to show his mom what he wanted. We also taught him how to use an "all done" bowl, where he could place something he didn't want to eat to reduce food waste. The "all done" bowl is an example of receptive communication, as it provides a designated space for something the child doesn't want. His expressive piece was physically moving the food into the bowl. His expressive skill improved from throwing food on the floor to placing it into the bowl.

We were working verbally as well, but the main mode of communication for him was visual. We used that throughout the house. He used to get frustrated when he wanted to go outside but couldn't. We used pictures and a stop sign to communicate to him that he couldn't go outside and to explain why—it's raining, it's too dark, or Mommy couldn't go right now. His mom also taped pictures of alternative options to the back door, such as playing with bubbles, crayons, different TV shows, blocks, and characters he liked. We started with just two of his favorite things to avoid overwhelming him and then built onto that to give him more options. Visuals provided a bridge for communication and made a huge difference in his life and that of his parents.

Visual cues are a form of nonverbal communication. We often naturally pair verbal and nonverbal communications together, such as picking up a sippy cup while asking, "Are you thirsty?" The visual of you picking up the cup helps the child pair "thirsty" together with the cup, even though that isn't the actual label for the object.

Why and When to Use Visual Support Cues

When children are learning the first steps of communication, we use visual cues such as pictures of items, people, activities, and locations. Sometimes, these cues are particularly helpful if your child is a visual learner who enjoys looking at books, people, and items. Some children are preverbal or nonverbal, and we need the language bridge to communicate more complex ideas. We could say, "Say goldfish!" many times, but if the child doesn't have those skills yet, it could be more effective for them to point to a picture of a goldfish or hand it to you. This is a first step and a bridge to verbal communication.

When preverbal children get exposed to visual cues, along with the word spoken by the caregiver, this helps reinforce the repeated vocabulary. When a word is merely spoken, it can disappear into the space around us because it doesn't have a concrete definition the way it does when it is used along with a visual cue. Pictures don't go away so quickly. This is one of the main reasons why reading board books to young children is such a fabulous tool for language acquisition.

Myths

The myths about visual cues are similar to the myths about bilingual learning. People outside of the SLP and behavior realms often think that visual cues are going to delay speech, but that's not true. Often, this bridge can help.

Pictures can bridge the gap across languages, too. I've found them to be immensely helpful when working with a child whose home language is not English.

ASHA has many resources on augmentative and alternative

communication (AAC). Visit the ASHA website for more information about the myths of AACs and visuals.[2]

Using Visual Cues at Home

Believe me, I could write an entire book on this subject alone! But you won't need to dive that deeply into visual cues unless your child has a learning difference that makes visual cues your main way of communication. For those who are using visual cues as a bridge between nonverbal and verbal communication, you'll introduce new pictures/visual cues one at a time building on your child's success. (If a dozen pictures showed up taped to the back door all at once, even a highly communicative adult may not understand why!)

If your child quickly grasps the concept that if they bring you a package of goldfish, you will open it for them, then the visual cues are likely to work well for them. You can print out pictures of things that are relevant to your child's life: their favorite activities, foods, toys, and so on. You can use these pictures strategically, such as the example of taping the reasons your child cannot go outside onto the back door, along with some alternative activities. Be sure to always pair your pointing at a picture with the words it represents. "It's raining."

For the items in your pictures, always have them readily available and only use pictures of things you can immediately honor. You can be creative with this! If you have a picture of Grandma, but Grandma isn't at the house, perhaps her picture can symbolize FaceTiming Grandma.

Onward!

We've covered a lot in part 1. You learned about developmental milestones, how to identify your child's strengths and opportunities to teach to those strengths, their current verbal skills, how to identify and address concerning behaviors, the importance of multilingual and bilingual learning opportunities in a nontraditional way, visual cues, and how you can engage in your child's language sessions if your child sees an SLP.

In the next section, we'll cover a little more ground before we get to the strategies, namely, how to identify your child's verbal level. You're ready to use the home-friendly strategies we'll discuss in part 2.

PART II

SPEECH AND LANGUAGE ACTIVITIES

CHAPTER 5

HOW TO USE THESE ACTIVITIES

This book focuses on the different verbal levels of children aged one to three years. It is geared toward building on a child's strengths and opportunities for learning at their particular stage in development, not specifically their age.

These strategies are designed to be incorporated into the natural daily activities you do with your child or children every day. You may already have a routine created for these activities, such as diaper changes. If you say, "Let's change your diaper," that means you go to the same space in your home; give your child a wipe, diaper, or toy to hold; sing a diaper changing song; put a diaper under them; get rid of the dirty diaper in the same way; and put the child on the floor to play or back to where you were before the diaper change.

TO LEARN MORE

To learn more about natural daily activities, I recommend the "Naturalistic Intervention" module from the National Professional Development Center on Autism Spectrum Disorders.[1]

It's so easy to incorporate one small change into these existing routines to create an amazing opportunity for language learning. In chapter 7, "Diaper Changes," you'll learn how effective it can be to do diaper changes in the bathroom, helping your child learn bathroom-related vocabulary and understand that the bathroom is where potty things happen.

Some of these strategies overlap and can be used throughout the day during different routines, such as labeling items, actions, and people, as well as incorporating visual cues into your daily routines.

But before we get to the activities themselves, there are a few more things to cover. Be sure to read it all, as many of the activities in the chapters to come will reference information from this chapter. In this chapter you'll learn how to use the activities in the chapters to come, as well as any necessary information, such as how to identify your child's verbal level. We'll discuss the importance of one of my favorite acronyms: SPOT, which refers to making an activity Specific through Positioning, identifying Opportunities, and Teaching.

Chapter Contents

Each activity described in the following chapters will encompass

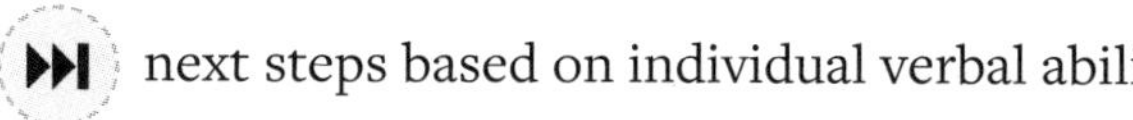

next steps based on individual verbal abilities;

a checklist for ease of using the strategies, including materials, preparation, and reflection;

FAQ; and

applicable case studies.

ACTIVITIES WITHOUT TECH

All the activities you will find in the following chapters are designed to be screen-free learning opportunities, although there will be small instances of perhaps using a photo on a smartphone as a visual cue. However, the child is not interacting with the phone for entertainment. The activities in this book include real toys or objects you may have around your house to encourage speech, language, play, social, and relationship-building skills.

The American Academy of Pediatrics recommends no screen time for children under the age of two and no more than one hour a day for children from two to five years old.[2]

Verbal Levels

We've probably all heard of a two-year-old who was basically speaking in full sentences or another kiddo who didn't use full sentences until they were over three. Children learn at different rates, whether or not they have a learning difference. (Milestones are a better indicator of potential learning differences than verbal levels are, so if you suspect your child may have a learning difference based on the milestone charts in chapter 1, I advise you to seek a professional opinion.) Because this book is for kiddos who may have learning differences and those who don't, I've structured the activities by verbal level rather than milestones. Learning differences do not change the approach for these strategies. As long as you're working within their verbal level, the strategies will be the same.

The verbal skills I reference throughout the book are in four categories: preverbal, verbal 1, verbal 2, and verbal 3. Unlike milestones, verbal levels are not based on age but rather the child's abilities. Each activity in the following chapters will be broken down by verbal level so you can best meet your child where they are in their language development.

The most important part of identifying your child's current verbal level is to help you understand what their potential next steps will be.

For example, if a child is at the preverbal level, using vowel sounds and gestures, and the caretaker is trying to get them to learn to say "More milk!" well, that's two words together, which would be going straight from preverbal to verbal 2, skipping over the verbal 1 phase. Even if the caretaker models "more milk" over and over, the reality is that the child needs time to catch up to the goal. This can frustrate everyone involved! Instead, we would focus on modeling one word such as "milk." More on that later.

If you identify your child's verbal level right now as you begin working through the activities in the book and then reevaluate monthly, you will be surprised at how quickly their language improves when you provide targeted speech and language learning opportunities while regularly acknowledging their accomplishments.

Let's look at each verbal level that appears in this book.

Preverbal

Much of a preverbal child's communication happens through body language, including the following:

- Handing you an item they need help with
- Pulling you to the kitchen to open the refrigerator
- Having tantrums
- Looking at you and using a consonant/vowel combination
- Pointing
- Crying

While some of these examples sound negative, they are all "communicative actions" that commonly occur in the preverbal stage.

If your child is displaying unusually concerning behavior, see the concerning behavior chapter for more information.

A preverbal child can also use vowel sounds and may be combining vowels and consonants. For example, you may hear "baa" for "ball." They may also combine these sounds with gestures, such as pointing or reaching for you to pick them up.

VERBAL 1

Children in this level put consonants and vowels together to make words and pair them with gestures. Basically, they're frequently using a single word when communicating.

Some examples include the following:

- Looking at you and saying, "Yogurt," to mean "Give me a yogurt" or an approximation of "yogurt" such as "gurt" only.
- Saying, "Up," when they look at you and put their arms up to mean "Pick me up."

To learn more about expanding on vocalizations (within all verbal levels), I recommend The Early Intervention Kit by Nancy B. Swigert.[3]

If your child is in the verbal 1 level, you'll be building on the words they already know, helping increase the complexity of what they can say. For example, if they say "ball," you might respond with "red ball."

If they say "wawa," you might say "water." (As tempting as it is to say "wawa" like they do, it isn't advised. Try to always model the correct way to say words.)

It's possible your verbal 1 kiddo can say "yes" and "no," which is great! But be aware that by asking too many questions that begin with "Do you . . . ," may create their first words of "Do" instead of the word of the item/person/thing that specifically communicates their need. I've worked with kids who thought every question had to begin with "Do you . . ." which is great they are imitating! Our first goal will be to add onto the "Do you" and teach the specific words so they can successfully communicate with others in their world.

VERBAL 2

These children are using two words together. Verbal 2 children usually have fifty words they're using consistently. (They don't have to be perfect words. "Wawa" for "water" counts.)

Your approach will include asking questions such as "Where are the toys?" You'll also add more words onto what they can already say. If they say, "Mommy, up?" you might respond, "Pick me up, Mommy?" (And then you pick them up. You aren't requiring a response from them, just reinforcing the language they shared with you and adding onto it.)

VERBAL 3

Verbal 3 children are using three or more words together. They've mastered using two- to three-word phrases and are consistently using sentences. Children in this stage usually are able to tell stories and retell events that happen to them with most of their listeners understanding more than 80 percent of what they say. Children in this stage still use word approximations. However, if they are not understood by an "untrained or unfamiliar" ear (someone who doesn't listen to this child regularly and who is not trained in speech and language development), advocate for them to be screened by an SLP.

A verbal 3 child already has a rapidly growing vocabulary, so you will be adding content such as sequencing, asking and answering questions, and storytelling. You can model full sentences at their level and prompt them to keep telling you about certain events, people, and things in their lives.

SPOT

SPOT is a collection of strategies aimed at teaching language to young children that should be implemented throughout the activities. SPOT stands for Specific, Positioning, Opportunities, and Teaching. Let's look at what each of these characteristics means.

Specific

Use **SPECIFIC** sounds, words, gestures, and phrases when you are setting up the learning opportunities for your child.

You may think, *Yes, I'm always using specific words with my child.* But you may be surprised at how often we tend to use general words/phrases, teaching them specific words which not only leads to more language learning opportunities but can also help you avoid communication breakdowns.

Here's a common example:

You've just made a lunch plate for your child. There were slices of cheese, grapes, carrot sticks, and yogurt. Your child was hungry, so they ate the whole lunch. You may see their empty plate and say, "More?"

They nod, smile, or maybe say (or sign), "More!" In this moment, we don't know what they want "more" of, so we get into this back-and-forth of "more cheese, more...so on." Instead we could model the words individually, teaching our kiddos to advocate for specifically what they want more of.

I've seen this happen a lot. Kiddos I'm meeting for the first time will walk up to me and sign "more." But I don't know what they're referring to. This can be frustrating for them and, at worst, can break down the confidence they have in their own communication skills.

You can be more specific at lunchtime by pointing to the food on their plate and modeling the words. Then if they ask you for "more," you could say, "More cheese?" Even if they can't say the word "cheese," they can communicate to let you know that's what they want.

You can absolutely teach your child the word "more." But it's best when they already know the words for specific items, which would put them at the verbal 1 to verbal 2 level.

Positioning

The **POSITION** of your body, face, and eyes in relation to your child's body, face, and eyes is important when it comes to language learning. You want them to be able to see you clearly, and ideally, you'd have their undivided attention. You want them to see your facial expressions and lip and tongue movements while speaking. This creates social learning opportunities that are imperative to language development.

Opportunities for Learning

This goal is to set up the activity to ensure you're creating the best possible learning opportunity. You'll want to ask yourself questions such as the following:

- Is my child ready for this activity?
- Is this a good routine to work into our lifestyle?
- Am I ready to meet my child where they are today?
- Do I have the materials I need?
- Is my child in a reasonably good mood today?

Teaching

We could spend a week together learning how to teach, and I have enjoyed being a part of weeklong seminars providing professional development to educators, families and practitioners. However, I know I can't give it that much detail here. Simply put, you'll need to learn to recognize individual strengths to lay the foundation for growth. This is why we need to identify their verbal level before attempting an activity and then build off it gradually.

Many of these activities are more or less the same for the verbal levels. It's *how you respond* that changes. Instead of just talking and talking to them, you're giving them one more word or one more phrase or one more communication skill to build off what they're giving you. We aren't simply exposing them to language. We're also using strategies to help them build their communication skills based on their existing skills.

Existing skills, such as gestures (body movements), that they are using to communicate are effective. You may not even notice your kiddo communicating with you! Preverbal children often miss out on so many language learning opportunities because so many adults don't recognize the communication they *are* doing. (My specialty is first words regardless of age, so I could go on and on about the value of this work for preverbal kiddos.)

Modeling versus Narrating

Narrating is just talking. You may be giving a specific word to expose your child to it, but you aren't trying to get them to imitate you, just exposing them to language. We typically do this all throughout our interactions with our children. While exposure to language is helpful, it is not as direct as modeling. The child can't often pick the important words out of a sentence.

Modeling is saying a word with the intention of having the child imitate it back to you. Let's say your goal at snack time was to teach the word "cup."

Make sure they're paying attention and looking at you so they'll associate the word with the item. You'll hold the cup and say, "Cup," and when they say something close to that word, you give the cup to them. Use the rule of three here but always give the item to them as soon as they imitate you.

The Rule of Three

Parents ask me all the time, "How many times should I repeat a word for them?"

There's really no one-size-fits-all answer here. But my usual answer is three. It is enough times that the child gets to hear the word repeated but not enough time that they get frustrated.

Imagine your child comes up to you, looking up with their arms extended. Their body language says, "Pick me up!"

You could pick them up. Or you could go for the trifecta of eye contact, gesture, and vocalization. So you say, "Up!" then pause. Repeat this two more times, picking them up as you say it for the third time.

(There have been situations where I've said it more than three times and times when I've skipped this when a kiddo was frustrated.) Watch their cues and be aware of shifting your expectations based on their current needs.

GOOD QUALITY RESOURCES

Throughout this book I will recommend good quality resources that you can access for free. To me, good quality means researched-based resources that I'm familiar with and I've used myself in practice with kiddos in my personal and professional life and have had success with. All of these links/resources were available when this book went to print. However, if any of these links do not work, email the Path for Words community at info@pathforwords.com, and we will provide you with an updated resource.

This book, and the whole Path for Words community, is focused on sharing good quality resources. The more you read and immerse yourself in teaching your child new skills such as speech, language, and play, the more you learn about your child and what's best for them as a person.

Checklists

It'll be clear to you as you get into the activity chapters that I love a checklist as much as I love a flowchart. There are checklists throughout the chapters to help you set up the activity and reflect upon it afterward. Our goal isn't that every single thing you do has a checklist! It's helpful to think about your goals before jumping into an activity as it builds intention. Over time, that just becomes part of your play.

Get Prepared

Don't worry, you can do this in two minutes. This is a bit of simple preparation to decrease your stress in the moment, *not* homework that will add to it.

- ☐ Know what verbal level your child is.
- ☐ Decide which caretaker is performing the activity.
- ☐ Collect your materials, including visual aids.
    - Pro tip: If these are toys or household objects, rotate them out on occasion so there's something new to discover.
- ☐ Think about what activity you want to attempt.
- ☐ Remember SPOT. You can choose one of these items as your goal, such as positioning, making sure your child is always face-to-face and can see your facial expressions and lip movements. It can be really effective to break it down rather than try to attempt all four strategies at once.

- [ ] If this isn't the first time you've used a certain activity, consider what went well last time and what might need to change (i.e., there were too many toys, or the child didn't like the toys). If you tried too many strategies at once, maybe back up and try one at a time, such as using very specific language.
- [ ] Communicate with other caregivers on an ongoing basis to let them know your current goals and learn about new skills your child may have demonstrated for other caregivers. (I recommend passing a notebook back and forth. I've worked with people who keep a group text thread or even use a shared Google Doc. I've seen people use sticky notes as well, leaving a goal word or skill written on the note and left in various places, such as the diaper changing table or the bathtub. I find that having this communication in writing is very helpful. Words can get lost in the air. When you have something you can look at and read, it really helps you stay on top of your goals. Whatever works for you and your child's team!)

A Note on Timers

You'll see "timer" noted in several chapters on the "materials needed" list. Timers are very helpful for some kiddos. I use them all the time in my sessions. When I mention "timers," I don't mean simply the timer app on your phone or an hourglass, though those could certainly work.

I tend to get creative with my timers, especially for children who benefit from visual cues. One of my favorite "timers" is a blank card with a few (six to ten) squares of Velcro on it. You'll have different characters (for this example, let's use Minions) cut out with the other side of the Velcro on it. As time passes, you have the child stick one of the Minions to the Velcro. When the last minion goes on the card, we transition into the next activity. Letting the child put the Minions on the card gives them a sense of authority in the activity. It's also a great visual tool of the card getting filled up, so they can see how much time is left.

TO LEARN MORE

To learn more about timers, you could check out "Visual Timers and Behavioral Management" by Caroline Scott.

This timer strategy is great for kids who both hate or love an activity. They can visualize it coming to an end, which helps them tolerate the activity for longer or helps them transition out of the activity with minimal stress.

One of my other favorite timers is the Visual Countdown Timer. It's a free app that visualizes a circle being completed as the time counts down, and once the timer goes off, the circle shows an image of the next activity (e.g., a popsicle, a toy, a person). You can change that picture to be something from your own photos so it could be their grandparent or their favorite toy.

If you're new to timers, it's a good idea to start by using them for a neutral activity, not your child's favorite but not something they hate, either. Introduce it to them and let them see what it represents: the passage of time and a reminder from something (not us!) that the activity is over. This can also be helpful to avoid them begging you to extend their time, as the timer itself is the authority. But be aware that you have to abide by the timer because as soon as you start overriding the timer, they'll realize they can appeal to you for more time after all.

At first, set the timer for short periods of ten minutes or under. You can use it for the final activity within a longer activity, such as the final five minutes of bath time. You don't need to use it for the entire time they're in the water. But you may graduate to that as your child learns to use it and what it signifies. Just start small and do what works for you!

We're always looking to make the activity more fun for the child while also helping them understand exactly what's going on. Timers can be excellent tools for that, and we want to make the timer itself as fun as possible.

"Grandma's Rule"

Sometimes, you have to do something you don't want to do before you get to do something you really want to do. We call this "Grandma's Rule." Grandma wouldn't let you eat a cookie before your dinner, would she?

I use this concept often when working with kiddos in sessions, my own little one and also when trying to accomplish my own personal and professional goals! "Save the best for last" is another way to think of it. This helps incentivize us to get through the first activity because you know something awesome is coming up next.

TO LEARN MORE

To learn more about Grandma's Rule, I recommend the article "Grandma's Rule; Cultivating Motivation" from the Housson Center.[4]

Grandma's Rule can pair nicely with a timer as well. If your child is refusing to eat dinner and just wants dessert, you could say, "We're going to eat vegetables for five Minions, then you can have dessert."

Or if they're struggling with bath time, you could say, "We're going to wash five different body parts (adding Minions along the way), and then you can have all of your toys in the water."

Whenever I talk about Grandma's Rule, I like to remind caregivers that it's hard to reinforce a skill with something the child doesn't particularly care for. If you've said you're going to put their favorite toys in the water after washing five body parts, but what you really do is just continue washing them, that's not going to incentivize them to participate in this activity. Sometimes, I make the analogy that if all of a sudden, your paycheck wasn't money but pizza, you'd be pretty mad, even if you like pizza. That wasn't the deal, was it?

Promise them something you plan to deliver, and promise them something they want to receive.

TO LEARN MORE

To learn more about reinforcement, I recommend the book *Parenting with Science: Behavior Analysis Saves Mom's Sanity* by behavior analyst Leanne Page.[5] It is full of amazing behavior strategies that will complement the strategies and activities in this book. In *Parenting with Science*, Page writes about the importance of reinforcement. (The **Play Is Work** breakout boxes are inspired by this book.)

Now that you know how to make your activities SPOT and how to identify your child's verbal level, you're ready to move on to the activities and routines themselves.

CHAPTER 6

BATH TIME

Why Bath Time?

Bath time is a wonderful time for language learning. Because it usually happens either daily or several times per week, it leads to repeated vocabulary exposure. The repetition gives us ample opportunities to build upon our kiddo's consistent words.

The caregiver's body positioning during bath time is perfect for face-to-face attention. This gives the child an uninterrupted view of their caregiver's facial expressions and mouth movements. Also, by nature, the caregiver is paying excellent attention to the little one while they're in water. The caregiver is immersed in the activity just as much as the kiddo. Joint attention is the first piece to language learning. You create a bubble and say, "Bubble!" and they are looking right at the bubble with you. Joint attention is necessary to be able to map the words we use onto the corresponding actions.

There's a social piece to the joint attention as well, where they learn the natural back-and-forth of shared language.

TO LEARN MORE

To learn more about joint attention, I recommend the article "10 Activities to Work on Joint Attention" from the Clubhouse.[1]

There is also an opportunity for you to model emotional regulation[2] and boundaries in a safe way. If you've asked not to be splashed and they splash you anyway, you can say, "Mommy doesn't want to be splashed. I will have to get a towel to dry myself."

Note: If your kiddo *hates* bath time, you may want to start with some of the other strategies. Don't skip this chapter completely, though. There are many parts to these strategies that can help you make bath time more fun, which, over time, can make it a great time for language learning.

GET PREPARED

This is the time to get prepared for this learning opportunity. Before you collect materials, make sure you've read through the "Get Prepared" section in chapter 5.

Materials Needed

You only need a couple of these materials at a time.

- ☐ Bath "toys" with language opportunities. (They don't have to be actual toys. They can be measuring cups, rubber spatulas, Tupperware containers, and so on—anything that's safe and waterproof.)
- ☐ Bubbles
- ☐ Bath crayons
- ☐ Bath Play-Doh
- ☐ Plastic toys—traditional bath toys or safe, waterproof household items. Don't underestimate a set of plastic or silicone measuring cups! You can use them to scoop and pour water, trap bubbles, and so on. You don't have to buy things to have fun!
- ☐ A container for the toys—a plastic tote or big Tupperware
- ☐ Timer
- ☐ Visual cues (if necessary), such as pictures of bath toys on your phone that might motivate them to want to take a bath

Activity Time

Activity 1: Toy Container

The very basis of this strategy is that if all the toys live in the bathtub all the time, there's little opportunity for structured language learning. If we keep the toys in a separate container, we can create lots of opportunities for language. Later in this section, I'll break it down specifically by verbal level.

You'll have the opportunity to let the child request a certain toy either verbally or through gestures or visual cues. Then the caregiver can add extra language input when introducing the toy. Rather than the toy simply being available from the beginning, now the caregiver can produce the rubber duck and say, "Yellow duck goes *splash*!" when dropping it into the water.

You can also work with toy groupings.

- "Do you want to play with animals or cars?"
- "Do you want to play with the red cups or the blue cups?"
- "Do you want to play with stars or blocks?"

Leverage the fact that they can choose the toys, giving them a safe and expressive place to make decisions and have them met. That motivates them to want to do bath time, which is a great opportunity for kids with concerning behaviors.

At the end of the bath, you can put everything back in the container and name it again, reinforcing the words your child heard during the bath. This can also be helpful from a behavioral standpoint for kiddos who love bath time and have a hard time when it's over. This can create a goodbye ritual, where they can say "goodbye" (or wave) to each toy at the end of the bath. They see where all the toys will be waiting for them next time.

PREVERBAL NEXT STEPS

Consider the sounds your child has already made. Maybe they can make a "puh" sound, so you can build on that by pouring water from a cup and saying, "Pour." Bubbles can "pop." Repeat the word several times so they can try to imitate you. (Imitation is expressive communication.)

Build upon gestures such as reaching and making eye contact. If they're reaching for something to signal that they want it, the next step is to make eye contact with the communication partner (the adult). It's the preverbal way to say "Hey, you, I'd like that." After the reach + eye contact, we'll try to get the trifecta of adding the verbalization as well. For children with different learning abilities and delays, this is one of the first steps we teach. If eye contact makes them uncomfortable, we find something else that works for them, such as scooting closer to their communication partner. We're not *forcing* them to make eye contact but providing the opportunity. For very little kids, this is a great way to add in a social part of this communication.

Here's an example of how this strategy could be used with a preverbal child:

The caregiver brings out the container and takes out two toys. She holds them up, pauses, and lets the child point to the toy they want. Then the caregiver says, "Cup!" or even a short full sentence, such as "You want the cup!" to model the language, and gives the child the cup, which gives them immediate feedback after their gesture and hearing the word modeled.

Here are some other things caregivers can do with preverbal kiddos:

- Make animal sounds (quack, woof, moo) to give the child the opportunity to use a vowel/consonant together.
- Make associated sounds such as "Boom!" when something lands in the water or the revving of a truck engine. If something falls over, say, "Uh-oh!" paired with a gesture. These are all cues for the child to imitate you.

- Pair actions with the objects. For example, you could put a measuring cup over your nose and "sneeze" it off. For a preverbal kiddo, it's easier to imitate "Achoo!" than to imitate actual words.
- Use mostly one-word modeling, such as "Duck!" However, still sprinkle in full sentences, even though you aren't expecting the child to imitate your sentence. "The duck is swimming!" is as complicated as it needs to be. (Language exposure is receptive communication.)

⏭ VERBAL 1 NEXT STEPS

Fill up the bathtub without toys, then ask the child to choose the toys they'd like.

(Remember to avoid using too many "Do you . . . ?" sentences. Try to vary your vocabulary by saying things such as "jump or swim" while making the bath toy do that action. You can introduce more "Do you . . ." questions once the child is in the verbal 2 level.)

They can request the toys by making noises or by gesturing, but we're trying to give them plenty of opportunities to use a word or an associated noise, such as "swish, swish, swish" for a swimming toy.

Add onto their phrases. If they say, "Cup," you can say, "Yellow cup."

Include possessive words, such as "your cup" or "my cup."

Introduce adjectives, such as "big cup."

Whatever they're saying, you can add another word to it, as long as it makes sense and is grammatically correct.

Here are some other things caregivers can do with verbal 1 kiddos:

- Label and model what we want to teach. Everything that comes out of your mouth is what you're teaching. Focus on the target word you want to hear them say, no matter what's coming out of their mouth.
- Work on location words. If they've asked for the duck, you can put the duck under the cup and say, "The duck is under the cup." This is adding onto the one-word label of the item. Remember, we aren't expecting them to mimic that sentence; we're just modeling what "under" means.
- Sing the cleanup song.

 VERBAL 2 NEXT STEPS

The caregiver models two- to three-word phrases, repeating them a few times, such as "The duck swims," encouraging the child to try putting these words together.

Add onto their phrase. If they say, "Yellow cup," you can say, "Pour with the yellow cup."

Introduce pronouns, such as "Your yellow cup."

Include people's names, such as "Daddy likes that purple cup."

Add action verbs using a person, such as "Let's show Daddy how we pour with the purple cup."

The child may only say, "Daddy," but you build off it. It's the same as verbal 1, but you're making it more complex.

Here is another thing caregivers can do with verbal 2 kiddos:

- Start introducing longer questions, such as the following:
    - "Do you want the animal who swims or the animal who runs?"
    - "Do you want to pour, or do you want to sing?"

- “Should we play with the cups or the singing star?”

VERBAL 3 NEXT STEPS

The caregiver’s model consists of three or more words, such as “The yellow duck goes splash!” Repeat two to three times to see if the child will mimic you.

A fun thing to do with verbal 3 children is to take items out of the container and tell a story about them. Let the child add to the story.

“This duck is going to swim in the ocean and find a fish. What is your duck going to do?”

Build off the child’s answers: “Wow, he’s going to build a sandcastle! Is he going to do that alone, or does he have any friends at the beach to help him?”

They already have a rapidly growing vocabulary, so you will be adding content, such as sequencing, asking and answering questions, and storytelling.

Activity 2: Modeling with Bath Toys

Particularly for bath time, there are many opportunities for modeling different vocabulary.

BUBBLES

Bubbles are great for this. “Pop!” is a great word and mouth movement. You can gesture to the bubble and follow it with your finger and eyes. You can say, “Up!” and “Down!”

Bubbles can land on body parts, giving you the opportunity to model those words, such as "Toes!"

There are so many verbs that apply to bubbles. You can blow bubbles, swish them, scoop them, or watch them float.

Unlike a toy, they disappear, and you can make them again, creating another opportunity for language.

 PREVERBAL NEXT STEPS

Just focus on the associated sounds and gestures. For example, say, "Pop!" Blowing bubbles off your hands is a gesture. This is great for back-and-forth sound games, which is a preconversation verbal back-and-forth. You might only be saying, "Ahh!" and other sounds, but if it's back-and-forth, it's creating the foundation for conversation.

 VERBAL 1 NEXT STEPS

Have them practice following a point by pointing at the bubbles. This doesn't sound like a big piece, but when they're following the point, they're able to associate a word to that item. Pair the word and item/action by saying, "Bubble."

They will learn to receptively understand what the word means.

 VERBAL 2 NEXT STEPS

You'll add more words to what they already know. This is a good time to introduce the idea of taking turns. "My turn to pop." Then give them a turn: "Your turn to pop." Encourage them to say, “My turn.” You know they’re able to say, “pop” and “bubbles” together, so this is a perfect opportunity for them to say. “My turn to pop.”

Other great words such as “again” and “more” are useful for verbal 2 because they can clarify what they want more of, such as “More bubbles.” (If you didn’t read the part of this book where I discourage teaching “more” and “again” without knowing other words, it’s because so many kids get frustrated when they ask for “more” without being able to specify what they want more of!)

 VERBAL 3 NEXT STEPS

You can give them three-step directions, such as “Get the bubbles and have your duck pop the bubbles.”

This is actually pretty complicated! They have to do three things: look at something, get two items, and then perform an action. That receptive language skill is powerful, and verbal 3 is ready for this.

BATH CRAYONS

Bath crayons are amazing for modeling colors. You can also engage in a question-and-answer format by asking, “What should I draw?” (You can also use visual cues here, such as toys of different shapes or cutouts, to stick to the shower walls.)

You can guess what the child is drawing, too. Perhaps they can answer with a yes or no, even nonverbally. If you throw in a funny guess, they might laugh.

PREVERBAL NEXT STEPS

Have them copy and imitate your actions. You can also imitate them. If they draw a circle, you draw a circle. See if they'll imitate you in return.

Use one word repetitively, such as "Dot, dot, dot, dot" (as you're drawing dots). This leads to imitating sounds and words and more communicative actions.

Say "Zoom" as you draw a long stripe down the side of the tub, along with other simple actions/sounds to pair with it.

You can also introduce emotional expressions by drawing a smiley/frowny face on the side of the bathtub. This is a great opportunity for songs, such as "If you're happy/sad and you know it . . ."

VERBAL 1 NEXT STEPS

They follow one-step directions, but the next step is adding a vocalization to the one-step direction, such as saying "Zoom" or "Up" *and* imitating the action. Build off that skill by combining a word with an action.

VERBAL 2 NEXT STEPS

Have them label the actions. They can say, "Zoom" when you draw your quick stripe. They might label movements and colors, such as "yellow up" or "blue down." They might say, "Blue face" when you draw a blue smiley, or they may tell you what to draw.

VERBAL 3 NEXT STEPS

Have them retell to another adult or child how they were playing with the crayons. Crayons aren't bath time–exclusive toys, so they can explain and demonstrate things while outside the bath in a different environment. You can prompt them by saying, "What shapes did you draw?" or "What colors did you use?"

BATH PLAY-DOH

Bath Play-Doh is great for making shapes. The verb opportunities are fantastic: pull, stretch, push, roll, ball, and so on. You can also model the names of the colors.

You can model some emotions as well: "It's so hard to push the Play-Doh against the tub. Oh no, it just broke! I have to make another one."

The verbal level breakdown for modeling simply follows the description of modeling in the previous chapter: You aren't inundating them with a string of new words. Instead, you're being strategic about the words you're modeling during an activity, and you're building onto their existing strengths.

PREVERBAL NEXT STEPS

You're going for one-step, simple imitated actions, such as squishing the Play-Doh.

You can do things to help spark interactions, such as giving them a container that's closed, so they have to communicate to get it open. You would model the word "help" or "open" when you open the lid for them.

⏭ VERBAL 1 NEXT STEPS

Add a word to the one-step, simple action. If you're squishing the Play-Doh, say, "Squish." If you're using a star-shaped cutout, say, "Star." Try to get them to imitate these words.

⏭ VERBAL 2 NEXT STEPS

Have them add words to actions. Label the actions as you do them and get the child to do the same. For example, say "Roll" while rolling and "Drop" while dropping a ball of Play-Doh.

⏭ VERBAL 3 NEXT STEPS

Have them tell you what they want you to make: cutouts, actions, and colors. Play-Doh can be recreated outside the bath as well, so like the crayons, they can tell another adult or peer about what they did with the Play-Doh.

Activity 3: Add New Items, Actions, or People

Here are some ideas for **all verbal levels**:

- Add new items such as a rubber spatula to the container from activity 1.
- Bring an "outside" water toy inside.
- Bring an unexpected object, such as a comb. "What is Mommy's comb doing in here?"
- Involve a new person such as a grandparent or caretaker. Usually, Mom does bath time, but tonight, Dad is doing bath time. The child might be very excited to show Dad

how the bath time routine goes and could get to practice some new words and add new pronouns. Verbal 3 kiddos could tell Daddy a story with the bath toys.

Activity 4: Songs with Gestures

The bathtub is an excellent place to make up songs or to sing songs you already know. One of my favorites is **"Clean up, clean up, everybody, everywhere!"** (Feel free to search it on YouTube if you've never heard it.) It not only teaches kids that activities come to an end, which is great for those who *don't* like certain activities and for those who *love* them but need to understand that the activity will end soon, but it also helps them transition out of an activity they don't want to end.

They clean up by placing their bath toys back in the container. You can practice modeling the names of the toys as they go into the container. For preverbal children, they can wave goodbye to the toys. With bath toys, this could involve scooping the toys into a container or putting the toys or materials into the container.

Another wonderful bath time song is **"Head, shoulders, knees and toes."**

At first, have the child touch their own body part as you sing about it. It's a different skill set to touch the body parts we can't see on ourselves, such as eyes, ears, mouth, and nose.

You can also sing about the caregiver's head, shoulders, knees, and toes, as well as different bath toys. It can be especially fun if the toy doesn't have the same body parts. For example, you might sing, "Head, shoulders, antlers, hooves, antlers, hooves!"

You can stray away from that song in particular and make up your own about your body: "Mommy's hair is long / is long. Baby's hair is short / is short." It doesn't have to rhyme or sound good.

Make up a song to a tune you know such as **"Frère Jacques"**: "He is walking. He is walking" as you're walking the character on the side of the bathtub. Then, "He is jumping. He is jumping. Watch him dive. Watch him dive."

PREVERBAL NEXT STEPS

This is their time to shine! They can contribute with gestures and facial expressions. **"If you're happy and you know it splash your hands!"** You can drip water on your face and make it look like tears for "If you're sad and you know it say 'boo-hoo'!"

Encourage them to make gestures with you, hum, or make vowel sounds to participate. The goal is to use one more gesture than they used the last time or to build on verbally, such as giving you a consonant/vowel combo.

You can model "surprised" by putting bubbles on your cheeks with your hands (such as Kevin with the aftershave in *Home Alone*). This is fun and easy for them to mimic.

They might have a song in their head but can't tell you what they want you to sing. If we can teach them how to link a gesture to a song, they can request a song. Or you can rely on visual cues.

Our goal is to have a social interaction and build receptive communication, such as singing the rubber ducky song and kid pointing to the duck.

VERBAL 1 NEXT STEPS

Have them sing or participate for one to two words within the songs. The goal is to add one word paired with a gesture, such as putting fists to eyes to indicate weeping when you sing “If you’re sad and you know it, cry out loud!” Then you could say, “If you’re . . .” and point to them to let them attempt to fill in the word “sad.”

They’re singing with you, adding words, and changing words to fit the scenario.

- Still labeling objects and actions.
- They can pick which songs they want you to sing.
- They can sing along and begin to adlib different lyrics as you “pass the mic” to them.

VERBAL 2 NEXT STEPS

Have them sing or participate for more words within the songs, continuing to pair words and gestures.

VERBAL 3 NEXT STEPS

They’re singing along with most of the words to the songs (assuming they’ve heard them before). The goal is for you to pause more than you would with the preverbal and verbal kiddos to let them sing more of it. You can also let them make up their own words to songs.

Reflection

This may seem overly simple, but it's easy to forget to reflect when you're a busy caregiver! After you form the habit of reflecting, you won't have to look at the checklist each time.

Take a brief opportunity for reflection. How did it go? Ask yourself some questions, such as the following:

- What can I do differently to make this easier for everyone next time?
    - Add or rotate toys.
    - Add visual cues.
- What communication did I observe? What am I building off next time?
    - Was there a new word or sound to celebrate? A new gesture/sound combination? Did they use a new word for the first time that you can build off next time you have this obstacle out?
    - Continue to celebrate these things next time.
- What skills should we practice more?
- What communication breakdown did we have?

FAQ

How do I know if my child is having fun?

I love this question. I ask myself this question all the time. I want my kiddos to have fun. It means that your goal is teaching, which is why you're concerned that the kid isn't having fun. Some kiddos let you know they like something by attending to you, looking at you, and engaging, but they may not be smiling or laughing. Maybe the cues that they like it have to do with how long they want to stay in the bath, not trying to get out.

How do I know if I should use this routine?

If this is a routine that goes really well, use the strategies and increase the complexity of your child's language. If everybody is struggling through this routine, this may not be the best learning environment. Try to make it a receptive learning opportunity, and that's it.

My child is exhibiting concerning behaviors during bath time. What should I do?

Don't skip bath time, but do make it quick. Knowing the bath time strategies can be helpful for you, but don't expect much from bath time. Especially at the beginning, it's important to use these strategies during times they enjoy.

That doesn't mean that bath time can't be a learning opportunity. Remember, protest words and negation are also important parts of our vocabulary. If they don't like bath time, the language learning opportunities might be more about protest words: *No! I don't like that!* The expressive language opportunity here is you naming the body parts, the kiddo protesting, and you using words to help them understand what they're feeling.

The receptive language piece involves their understanding of what we're going to clean next. Use visual cues, such as pictures of body parts, to mark off what's clean (head, chest, tummy, arms, legs). Then the goal can shift to toys or other items.

Case Study

I worked with a kiddo who *really* hated baths. He didn't mind water in general and enjoyed splashing and playing in kiddie pools and water from the hose. He also enjoyed playing with toys in the bathtub, but he hated being washed, especially his hair. Obviously, he needed to be washed from time to time!

We taped a laminated image of a little boy to the shower wall so he could point to which body part he wanted washed first: arms, legs, or feet. As each part was cleaned, he marked it on the image with a marker.

He got to see the progress and feel the satisfaction over choosing which body part to wash. Then he learned that he got washed very quickly when he didn't resist, and immediately after the hair was done, he got his toys, and it was playtime.

This kiddo only had vowel and consonant sounds at this time. He responded well to the predictability of the routine and learned many new words as he started to tell his mom verbally what he wanted washed first.

Bath time transformed from a complete struggle into a fun learning experience for this family!

REMEMBER: PLAY IS WORK

When I was in school studying speech therapy, I learned that the childhood development psychologist Jean Piaget believed that the work of a child is play, and play is the work of a child.

This idea has stuck with me throughout my career. Each session I walk into and each child I interact with, I try to remember that these “play” interactions are work for them. Learning takes a lot of energy! And just because we make it fun doesn’t mean it isn’t exhausting and often frustrating.

When it comes to bath time, remember that just before bed may not be the most conducive time for your child to learn. Adults can be quite rigid with our schedules. If your kiddo is struggling to engage during your bath time activities, take a step back and reflect if this is the best time of day to do it. They may be too tired right before bed.

TO LEARN MORE

To learn more about play as work, I recommend chapter 10 of *Parenting with Science: Behavior Analysis Saves Mom’s Sanity* by behavior analyst Leanne Page.

CHAPTER 7

DIAPER CHANGES

Potty trained? Skip this chapter and go on!

Why Diaper Changes?

Diaper changes happen multiple times every day, which lends itself to repetition and reinforcement of vocabulary. Teaching vocabulary around the routine itself sets the kiddo up for success once you start to potty train. They'll understand what poop and pee are, as well as words such as "wet" and "clean."

The positioning is face-to-face, and there is a lot of opportunity for focused attention. You have their attention much like bath time. You can make facial expressions while changing them.

GET PREPARED

This is the time to get prepared for this learning opportunity. Before you collect materials, make sure you've read through the "Get Prepared" section in chapter 5.

Materials Needed

- ☐ Diapers
- ☐ Wipes
- ☐ Diaper cream (whatever your child needs at that moment)
- ☐ A container of toys they can easily and safely hold (Your heads are very close, and they can easily hit you or themselves in the head, so make sure the toys are soft, easy to hold, and easy to clean.)
- ☐ Visual cues, such as toys they will get afterward (or pictures of these toys)
- ☐ A doll and diaper for verbal 3 children who may lead us through a sequence by changing the doll's diaper

Activity Time

Activity 1: Change in the Bathroom

Everyone else in the house goes to the bathroom *in the bathroom.* It's only the little ones who go potty elsewhere. If it's at all possible in your home, I recommend performing diaper changes in the bathroom whenever you can. This is often very helpful for potty training readiness, as they've learned to associate the bathroom with elimination. They'll also get exposed to more bathroom vocabulary simply from being in the space, though you can make it a goal to model the vocabulary purposefully.

⏭ PREVERBAL NEXT STEPS

Exposure to bathroom vocabulary in a receptive way as you model the words for them: diaper, wipes, toilet, sink, and so on. We may use these things every day, but we aren't always narrating the activities while we do them! You can teach them to understand the words "go potty" and how that corresponds to the bathroom.

If diaper changes can be tricky for you, you might opt to give them a toy while you change them. They can also choose their own toy. You can still communicate with them, make eye contact, and make plenty of facial expressions.

If they're making a vocalization of a vowel sound such as "ayeeee" for "diaper," your next step would be adding a gesture with it, such as having them hand you a diaper. You will still pronounce the word "diaper" correctly.

The action of giving the diaper or wipes to you is a communication. Teach them that this means that you will change their diaper. Some preverbal kiddos will use hand as tools and lead the caregiver to the diaper changing station or the bathroom to communicate what they need. You can help them learn to use their hands as tools.

⏭ VERBAL 1 NEXT STEPS

They can get involved with the routine by following one-step directions, such as walking into the bathroom, helping pull the shorts or pants down, and choosing the diaper. Receptively, they're learning that they're a part of this process. The diaper is now something they're responsible for, getting more independent during the routine while labeling with one word such as "diaper, or pull."

They're learning to expressively communicate things, such as saying, "Wet."

You'll build off their language. If they say, "Wet," you say, "Wet diaper" or "Your diaper is wet."

If they say, "No diaper!" you might say, "No diaper, dad." You can honor what they said by offering something to give them a choice in the matter. Offer a couple of toys to choose from or give them two more minutes with the activity they are currently playing. Such as, if they are playing with their blocks you can say "one more minute with your blocks, then we're changing your diaper."

⏭ VERBAL 2 NEXT STEPS

For their verbal participation, you'll do the same as verbal 1, except adding more words to theirs.

On the receptive side of things, they'll start understanding more about what's going on in the bathroom. You might explain to them how Mommy and Daddy use the toilet.

You can also try to get them to talk to you about something that happened during their day or about the toy they chose for the diaper change.

VERBAL 3 NEXT STEPS

Now they're able to tell you when they need a diaper change. From there, build off what they're saying to add complexity. If they say, "I'm wet," you can build that to "Your diaper is wet, so let's change it."

Give them the opportunity to talk about a video or book they've seen where a character gets a diaper change, becomes potty trained, or uses the bathroom. Let your kiddo tell you the story with their own words. Daniel Tiger is one of my favorites for this. Elmo has some appropriate books, too. A big part of potty training is spending time in the education phase of getting ready for learning these new skills.

Other things you can do with verbal 3 kiddos are as follows:

- Try to get your kiddo to talk you through the diaper change. Say, "I forgot how to change your diaper! I don't know what to do! Can you teach me how to change your diaper?"
- You can start more simply with questions, such as "Where are the wipes?" (You wouldn't do this every single time—one diaper change per day will be sufficient.)
- They can also walk you through the diaper changing routine with a doll, which is a beautiful way to add complexity to their understanding and their expression.

Activity 2: Changing Box

Note: This activity is more or less the same for all the verbal levels. It's your participation that will change based on their verbal level. For this reason, I'm only breaking down the verbal levels in the "Next Steps" section, not for the activity itself.

Much like the bath time container, the changing box becomes a motivation piece in and of itself. You'll collect some toys your child can play with and hold during diaper changes. (Remember, they should be soft, safe, and easy to clean!) This routine happens often, so the toys need to be fun. They don't have to be new and can be objects from around the house as well.

You'll also have the diaper changing necessities in the box, such as diapers, wipes, and powders/creams. The child will have the opportunity to choose and handle these items, too.

- Give them a bit of autonomy in the diaper change. You can give your little one a choice between two diapers, perhaps with different designs on them. You can also ask them to hand you the wipes and powder. The more involved they are, the more language they're exposed to as well. When they choose the diaper they want, you can model the language by saying, "The diaper with moons on it!"
- If diaper changes are challenging for them, you can let them choose a toy to play with after the diaper change is over. This can be done verbally (if they can speak about the toy) or through visual cues such as pictures. This is known as "Grandma's Rule."
- Choose a word you want to teach, such as "diaper" or whatever toy they're playing with. Pay attention to their sounds, mouth movements, and facial expressions. Diaper changes are a great opportunity to observe their nonverbal communication skills because they happen so often in a day.

Other activities you can incorporate during diaper changes are as follows:

- **"Where did it go?"** Introduce an item to them and then "lose" it. "Where is it? Under you? On your head? On your toes?" This is an opportunity for them to receptively learn body parts or to practice saying them if they're able.
- You can **let them choose the location** of the diaper change. They could choose between the floor or the diaper changing table. Using language to let you know where the diaper change will happen is the main point.
- **Adding visuals.** Let the child know what they're going to do afterward, such as by showing a picture of them playing "ticking clock" (or any game) with Dad or a picture of the trampoline. Whatever comes next can help motivate them to engage with you through the diaper change or at least not fight you every step of the way if they are resistant to diaper changes.

PREVERBAL NEXT STEPS

Start by giving them a choice between two items or pictures. Sometimes, It can be overwhelming to have more than two choices. They can reach or point to the one they want. That gesture is communicating what they want to come after the change, which helps avoid communication breakdowns, as the child can choose the toy they want.

⏭ VERBAL 1 NEXT STEPS

Build off their words by describing what they currently have in front of them. They say, "Car," you say, "Red car."

⏭ VERBAL 2 NEXT STEPS

Continue building the complexity. Now their "red car" is "fast red car" or "bright red car."

⏭ VERBAL 3 NEXT STEPS

You can ask them to tell you about the toy in their hands or about something that happened to them that day. You can ask for instruction/clarification, even getting funny about it. "Does the diaper go on my head? Or on your bottom?"

Reflection

- Did you use everything you grabbed? If not, you might not need all the materials.
- What can I do differently to make this easier for everyone next time?
    - Have a different toy for them to hold.
- What communication did I observe? What am I building off next time?
    - Was there a new word or sound to celebrate? A new gesture/sound combination? Did they use a new word for the first time that you can build off next time you have this obstacle out?
    - Continue to celebrate these things next time.

- What skills should we practice more?
- What communication breakdown did we have?

FAQ

What can I do if my kiddo doesn't like diaper changes?
Set a goal of changing concerning behaviors into communication during the diaper routine. Allow for safe ways for them to express that they don't want to have the diaper change. Obviously, the diaper has to get changed, but we want to diffuse the stress and frustration around it. I recommend setting a timer for two more minutes of play before going into the bathroom for the diaper change or by focusing them on choosing the activity for afterward.

Case Study

I worked with a verbal 1 kiddo who absolutely *hated* diaper changes. It took the family so long to get his diaper changed that it felt like they were happening all day long, strung together by concerning behaviors.

We started our approach by being flexible about where the diaper change took place. He got to choose as a way to make it a little more fun for him. (Ideally, diaper changes will happen in the bathroom, but if you're struggling to make them happen at all, you do what you have to do.)

We used visual cues to set up visualization of Grandma's Rule. He would see a picture of a fresh diaper followed by a picture of a toy car. He started to understand that after his diaper change, he got to play with the car.

Once he started to understand the system, we added more choices. His mom gathered his cars and toys into a bin, called the "diaper bin." While he got his diaper changed, he could look through the pictures of the toys in the bin. After the change, he got to get into the bin. There was also a picture of him playing a game with his dad, which was something he could choose when his dad was home.

He responded so well to this approach that he even started talking about cars and picking up car vocabulary, which he would often share with his caregiver while they changed his diaper.

REMEMBER: PLAY IS WORK

Sometimes, we have to shift goals to be realistic. Maybe yesterday your verbal 3 child walked you through the steps of the diaper change, but today they won't even hand you a diaper. It's okay. Just try to make it fun and make it out of there. I like to think, *Right now, it's too hard.* That doesn't mean it won't be available again tomorrow.

Try to meet your child where they are right now and have flexible goals. Perhaps all they need now is a big hug from their favorite stuffed animal, and that animal can sit in on the next diaper change. Work is easier to do when it's fun!

TO LEARN MORE

To learn more about play as work, I recommend chapter 10 of *Parenting with Science: Behavior Analysis Saves Mom's Sanity* by behavior analyst Leanne Page.

CHAPTER 8

SNACK TIME

Why Snack Time?

Snack time is unique in that it still involves the natural motivation to eat, but it is not a regular mealtime where nutrition is so integral. They probably aren't very hungry because they've already eaten a meal, but this is a great time to practice working with other foods and social back-and-forth. The pressure is off, so to speak. (You can also use toys to model trying new foods without putting pressure on your child to also try the food if they are a picky eater.)

Eating is social as well, so it's natural to chat while eating. They can pick up new play and social skills.

The positioning is also excellent, as you get to be face-to-face. There's a lot of focused attention either on you or on the food.

GET PREPARED

This is the time to get prepared for this learning opportunity. Before you collect materials, make sure you've read through the "Get Prepared" section in chapter 5.

Materials Needed

- ☐ Cookie cutters
- ☐ A beet or whatever is the goal food (strawberry, banana, etc.)
- ☐ Toddler knife (if applicable and for soft foods only)
- ☐ Wet napkin or towel to wipe it off

Activity Time

Activity 1: Body Stamps

Body stamping can be so much fun! It's a great way to introduce different foods or experience a familiar food in a different way. You just need to use cookie cutters as stamps to create fun, simple shapes with a beet. (Cook the beets as appropriate for your child's development. Plus, if your kiddo wants to eat it, they won't have trouble biting through it.) You can also cut the beets with a knife.

Then you'll use this little stamp to make a "tattoo" on your child's arms and hands. They can request shapes and decide where they want the stamp.

I like using sliced strawberries as well, though they don't

have as much color. I also use "banana kisses" by lightly touching a bit of banana to a kid's hand or arm. There's just a little bit left on their arm, so you can see where it was. Bananas are nice because they don't leave a stain, and some kiddos don't like stains. For others, that's the best part! When I say that you know your child best, that's what I mean. If you know they would not like the beet stain on their skin, try a banana instead.

TO LEARN MORE

To learn more about body stamps, I recommend *Broccoli Boot Camp: Basic Training for Parents of Selective Eaters* by Keith E. Williams, PhD, and Laura J. Seiverling, PhD.[1]

 PREVERBAL NEXT STEPS

This is a great opportunity for facial expressions: "Wow!" or "Uh-oh!" if you drop a piece.

You can also use the stamps on paper for additional engagement with this activity. The child can color in the stamp or draw a picture of the strawberry. While the child colors the stamp, the caregiver can recount what happened at snack time with the strawberry stamp.

 VERBAL 1 NEXT STEPS

You can have a goal to teach a word that either names or describes the foods: "Red," "Nana," or "Beet."

If you're using the coloring/paper stamp activity, the child can provide some details for the story, such as where the stamp was on their body.

VERBAL 2 AND 3 NEXT STEPS

Try to expand on what they can already say, such as "Banana kisses," "Body stamps," or "Put red on my hand."

For the paper stamp activity, the child can provide more details about the stamp experience and perhaps explain it to another caregiver.

Activity 2: Following Meal Prep Directions

Helping with meal preparation is one of my favorite activities for language learning. The possibilities for receptive language are endless. Plus, it can help neutralize situations with food for children who don't enjoy mealtime because there's no pressure to eat the food. (You can also have them help prepare something that they will eat.)

The child gets to imitate you, which is the foundation of learning new sounds, words, phrases, and gestures. Meal prep also introduces them to words they may not hear otherwise throughout the day, such as "mix" and "loaf." It's also a wonderful activity to help them build independence.

There are so many activities you could do for meal prep, but I'm going to focus on following directions. Let's imagine you're preparing a PB&J. (Obviously, if your kiddo can't eat peanut butter, just substitute whatever they can eat into this scenario. The food itself doesn't matter.)

⏭ PREVERBAL NEXT STEPS

Walk them through every step: going to the pantry to get the bread, how to step up onto the stool at the counter, and how to open the loaf of bread. Have them imitate one step at a time. There's no expectation here that they will be of any help or that they'll really understand what you're doing today. This is an opportunity for receptive language that you will build off.

Say things such as "Could you go get the bread?" Then show them exactly how to do that. There might be more steps involved that you didn't think about, such as opening a pantry door. Make sure you model everything for them so they don't get discouraged.

⏭ VERBAL 1 NEXT STEPS

Verbal 1 kiddos can follow a single-step direction without you modeling it. They should be able to retrieve an item without much help from you.

Say, "Could you go get the bread?"

Then once they've brought the bread to you, give them the next instruction.

⏭ VERBAL 2 NEXT STEPS

You can give them two instructions at once: "Go get the bread and put it on the table." Continue to give them two-step instructions as long as it makes sense to do so.

VERBAL 3 NEXT STEPS

Ask them to give you directions. They've made this PB&J several times, so now they can instruct you. This can be really fun, not only to see how much they've learned but also to make them laugh by being very literal.

For example, if they say, "Put the peanut butter on the bread," you can put the whole jar onto the slice of bread and make a face. Some kids find this hilarious. It also gives them an opportunity for more specific language when they have it, or you can help them fill in the gaps.

Reflection

- Did they react positively to the activity/food presented?
- What can I do differently to make this easier for everyone next time?
    - Add a different food.
    - Add a visual element as needed.
- What communication did I observe? What am I building off next time?
    - Was there a new word or sound to celebrate? A new gesture/sound combination? Did they use a new word for the first time that you can build off next time you have this obstacle out?
    - Continue to celebrate these things next time.
- What skills should we practice more?
- What communication breakdown did we have?

FAQ

How do I know if my kiddo is enjoying the activity?

Sometimes, when we're using new foods, it can be daunting for all of us.

It's important to watch their body language, smiles and the increase in their language. I've worked with some who are more subtle with their reactions; each child is unique. Like adults, kids can have varying reactions to something.

They can still have opportunities for language learning with the food we're using. Just stamp your own hand if they don't like it. It's important to shift the learning goal here. Instead of stamping them, let them watch you. Or let them help you put things away. That counts! (It's still using gestures to communicate.)

How do I know the next step?

We are always building off what they're giving us. That's why we break it down by verbal level. If they're saying, "Nana," the next step will be modeling "banana" only and adding a word onto nana. "My banana," "Your banana," or "Banana stamp."

Write it down to help you remember the progress. Your notes/notebook can also be passed between you and other caregivers so they can pick up where you left off. The difference between "cookie," "a cookie," and "a big cookie" is substantial! It's a big deal to use a new word or phrase with someone else, and if they forget to report it to you, you wouldn't know. It doesn't sound like it's a big deal for them to say "a cookie" with another caregiver if they've only used it with you, but it is!

Case Study

Here is an example of a kiddo I worked with who enjoyed strawberries, blended in smoothies, and we gradually created a snack option of the strawberries for him. We cut the ends off a fresh strawberry and used it as a body stamp to gradually introduce him to the food. This made the food new to him in a way that made him willing to try it. After it "stamped" his hand and he saw the little ring of pink on his skin, he was willing to try it. And (unsurprisingly, since we already knew he liked the taste!) he ended up loving strawberries in their raw form as well.

Something important about this approach was that we didn't do this during a structured meal, where he felt pressured to eat the strawberry. Letting him touch it first and explore it in a pressure-free environment really helped.

REMEMBER: PLAY IS WORK

Celebrate small moments, no matter how small, such as looking at a new food or saying, "No, thanks!" Communicating via facial expression is still communication. When their facial expression says "No," we have to let that be the language learning opportunity. The kiddo is still working hard to let us know what they want and need.

TO LEARN MORE

To learn more about play as work, I recommend chapter 10 of *Parenting with Science: Behavior Analysis Saves Mom's Sanity* by behavior analyst Leanne Page.

CHAPTER 9

RESTAURANTS

Why Restaurants?

Social eating is a major way we spend time together as humans—and that means humans of all ages! But often, it can be challenging to take our children to restaurants. I've heard so many parents tell me that they were *scared* to take their children to a restaurant. I totally understand! Many restaurants are simply not set up to be fun, inclusive spaces for toddlers. On top of that, many toddlers don't understand what's expected of them at restaurants.

The activities and strategies in this chapter will also encompass any meal that happens in an unfamiliar space, including eating at a friend's or family member's house.

While this chapter does offer many language learning strategies for social eating situations, it also offers some behavioral tips so you can keep your kiddo happy and engaged (screen-free) and enjoy your own meal as well. Simply learning to be in this social dining setting will be an enormous amount of communication input for your little one, from having the opportunity to overhear other people, watch you communicate with the server, and maybe even get to order for themselves. We'll break it down into baby steps so you can build on your child's existing skills and soon feel confident enough to go out to eat—without having to hire a babysitter!

GET PREPARED

This is the time to get prepared for this learning opportunity. Before you collect materials, make sure you've read through the "Get Prepared" section in chapter 5.

Materials Needed

Gather the materials listed below in a "restaurant bag" so they're always together. It's like a diaper bag—when you leave the house, it's all you have with you. Many of these items are particular to this chapter, and their larger definitions and purposes will be described at length further on.

- ☐ Picture supports to break down the restaurant routine
- ☐ Picture schedule (details within the activity)
- ☐ Timer
- ☐ Conversation mat (details within the activity)
- ☐ Communication board (details within the activity)

- ☐ Toys they can use at the table: crayons, coloring books, books, and toys that are small enough to be on the table (Don't bring things with a lot of pieces—even crayons. I'd suggest bringing only a few. Less is more!)
- ☐ Sticky notes (You can make impromptu timers out of them by drawing little boxes on them. You can check off/color in boxes every two minutes while waiting for food and so on. You can also draw a communication board or picture schedule on them if, for some reason, you don't have your other one. You can play with them, too.)
- ☐ Anything your child has had success with at a restaurant in the past

Activity Time

Activity 1: Communication Board

If you've ever traveled to a country where you don't speak the language, chances are, you ordered from the server by pointing at the menu.

Well, we're giving our preverbal kiddos a chance to do just that and giving the verbal 1–3 kiddos a chance to visualize what's on the menu and prepare to speak to the server.

This is a board, no bigger than a place mat, where you will put pictures of different items the restaurant has, different people we can talk to, and some toys that are in the restaurant bag. This is an opportunity for them to visually see their options and talk to you about it. The conversation can range from the different foods to requesting different activities available in the restaurant bag.

TO LEARN MORE

To learn more about communication boards, I recommend "Augmentative and Alternative Communication (AAC)," available on ASHA's website.[1]

They can also use it while ordering from a server, which can be a lot of fun for all verbal levels. The preverbal kiddos can point to the picture or hand the server the picture. A lot of times, the server will reply to them, giving them the chance to experience a new communication partner. This is a built-in opportunity for social language and social realities.

This board clearly explains what options are available to them, which helps prevent a communication breakdown. If you're at a Mexican restaurant (a favorite at our house!), you probably have pictures of a quesadilla, tacos, or an enchilada. But if your child doesn't know they don't serve pasta at that restaurant and tries to get pasta, that could set the scene for a communication breakdown or even a concerning behavior. This can ensure they understand their options available.

You can absolutely use these at other people's houses as well, though it may not be for the choice in food as much as the choice of activity. They now have a say in what they want and have an opportunity to communicate it rather than us anticipating their needs.

Note: It's important that your child is familiar with the communication board before their first restaurant experience. Otherwise, they won't understand what's expected of them! See the "Practicing at Home" activity.

⏭ PREVERBAL NEXT STEPS

You'll be exposing them to a lot of language in a restaurant setting, but have a specific goal in mind. Let's say your goal is that they tell you what they want to eat. When they point to the picture of french fries or look intently at the picture of fries, you might say, "Fries. Fries." Gradually give them the opportunity to repeat it. They might just make a long "I" sound first.

For their opportunity to communicate with the server, point at the server and have their communication board in front of them. They can point at the board or give the picture to the server. The whole idea is that they're looking at the server and have shifted their body to indicate the new communication partner.

Sometimes, you'll have to help out, but try to encourage this type of communication.

⏭ VERBAL 1 NEXT STEPS

Your child looks at the communication board and says, "Fries!"

You could reply, "Woah! French fries!" adding one word more than they gave you.

For their opportunity to communicate with the server, be flexible. They might just say, "Fry!"

You might say, "I want fries!" to give them the words they want.

⏭ VERBAL 2 NEXT STEPS

Your child says, "French fries!"

You add one word, saying something like "Big/curly/yummy/my french fries."

For their opportunity to communicate with the server, add a few extra words.

"I would like french fries."

WHEN TO SAY "PLEASE?"

Families often ask me when they should try to get their child to say "Please" and "Thank you." If those are words that your family uses, you can teach them in verbal 2/3 as soon as they're stringing two to three words together. Same with other polite words, such as "Yes, ma'am," or "No, sir." But this all depends on the family and whether these are valuable words for the kiddo to use.

In terms of pure language learning, I think giving a child a carrier phrase, such as "I want" or "I need," is more important to communication than "please" or "thank you." However, communication is highly personal, and if words such as "please" are important for your family or your culture, that's all you need to know!

VERBAL 3 NEXT STEPS

They say, "My french fries!"

You could say, "Yes, you're eating your french fries!"

Location words are fun with food as well: behind, beside, next to other food. You can ask them who has what food where. This is quite a bit more advanced than just requesting things. (If they don't enjoy mealtime routines or the outing, this may not be your priority—you may just be focusing on their food alone.)

For their opportunity to communicate with the server, they will use more complex language.

They might say, "I like french fries," but then pick up the chicken picture.

You say, "I like french fries, but I want chicken instead," helping them express this more complex idea. They've made a comment, and you're commenting on that comment.

Activity 2: Picture Schedule

The picture schedule is a picture representation of each step or each item in our restaurant outing or dining experience at someone else's house. I like printing out pictures, but I know that's not easily available for all families. You can use pictures on your phone if that's more reasonable for you.

This is an order of events with a picture or object representation of these basic events:

- First we sit down
- Order food
- Color a picture
- Look at the conversation mat (described in the next activity)
- Put some Minions on the timer
- Eat
- Get into the car (perhaps there are toys in the car to have pictures of)
- Go home (pictures of toys/pets/people at home)

This strategy shifts over time and can eventually be written words once they've learned to read. This sets them up for success later on.

(It's important that your child is familiar with the picture schedule before their first restaurant experience. Otherwise, they won't understand what's expected of them! See the "Practicing at Home" activity.)

SOMEONE ELSE'S HOUSE

It may feel odd to text your friend who invited you over for dinner to ask for a picture of their dining room table, but it can ultimately be a big relief for the host when your kiddo shows up feeling confident. You can ask the host for help with this piece without going overboard. Consider asking a picture of the host, where the eating will take place, perhaps a picture of the dish they intend to make, and, if applicable, a picture of something like an outdoor space they may get to use or the activity you've brought for them to play with.

Just ask yourself, What events are going to happen for the child? What will your child do? Go through it just like for a restaurant.

Activity 3: Conversation Mat

This is a sheet of paper with images of people, characters, animals, and toys that they really like that sits on the table in front of them. (I like to laminate it, use tape or put a plastic mat on top of it.) The conversation mat gives them the opportunity to initiate a conversation with us about whatever items are on there. Words get lost, especially in high-stimulation environments such as restaurants. This can also help them think of people or objects they don't see often. A picture of Grandma can prompt your child to talk about Grandma, even though she lives in another state. Preverbal kids can point at the images to get you to talk about them.

Mealtime is a great opportunity because we need a filler activity while they're sitting, waiting on the food. Back-and-forth conversation is a wonderful filler because that's probably what they'll be doing for the rest of their lives while waiting for food at a restaurant.

Caregivers can also benefit from this by streamlining how to interact and what to talk about. You don't have to bring every toy with you. You can just have a picture of the toy for conversation purposes. You can mime playing with it, such as drumming or playing a flute. When they point to a picture of a lion toy, you can pretend to be a lion. The possibilities are endless here. Just have fun with it!

(It's important that your child is familiar with the conversation mat before their first restaurant experience. Otherwise, they won't understand what's expected of them! See the "Practicing at Home" activity.)

NEXT STEPS

The next steps are very similar to the communication board. For preverbal kiddos, you'll encourage them to pair gestures and sounds together for more complex communication, such as pointing to the picture of the lion toy and going, "Rawr!"

For verbal 1–3, you're building on their existing words, adding slight complexity each time.

You can switch out the conversation topics every so often based on your goals and to keep things interesting.

Activity 4: Practicing at Home

This one can be really fun and an excellent opportunity for language learning and teaching those confidence-boosting societal skills that will help your kiddo know what's expected of them at the restaurant. You want to make the restaurant as unsurprising an environment as possible, and preparation can really help with that.

To do this activity, have your communication board, picture schedule, and conversation mat on the table or surface where your family usually eats, or if you have another dining surface that is a little less known to your child, that can work well, too. Use these materials as you would at a restaurant. Talk your kiddo through the steps of being at a restaurant, including communicating with the server.

It can be fun to pretend to be the server or to let another family member play that role so your child can watch you order food and then take a turn.

A verbal 3 kiddo might want to pretend to be the server too, which is an amazing opportunity for language learning.

Reflection

- What can I do differently to make this easier for everyone next time?
    - Add to the picture schedule or conversation mat.
    - Bring another activity.
- What communication did I observe? What am I building off next time?
    - Was there a new word or sound to celebrate? A new gesture/sound combination? Did they order for the first time?
    - Continue to celebrate these things next time you go out.
- What should we practice at home more? What communication breakdown did we have? What skills do we need to practice at home before we go back?

FAQ

I tried taking my toddler to a restaurant, and I'm scared to go back.

I always ask, "What happened? Give me the play-by-play. If you had to choose only one thing that you would change and one thing that you are proud of, let's focus on building off that."

He walked into the restaurant by himself. That's great! Let's build off that. We're going to walk into the restaurant with your restaurant go bag or something from it.

Just like with language, we want to build off their existing skills.

The idea is not to try to change everything all at once; we shouldn't put that pressure on ourselves. Have one thing to practice at home or one new skill to teach them and build off their strengths. Go for a shorter amount of time at a restaurant at a time when it isn't busy. Take the distractions away. Go to the same restaurant all the time.

 Case Study

I worked with a two-and-a-half-year-old named James who did not like going to restaurants. He exhibited several concerning behaviors when he went, and his parents soon became afraid to bring him to a restaurant. However, going out to eat was an important bonding experience for his family.

We started slow. Everyone else acts like they know exactly what's going on, but if you're a toddler, this is probably very confusing! There often aren't any toys, the high chairs are confining, and the place is unfamiliar, but you're not allowed to explore it. It can be really loud, too!

The first thing we did was learn how to walk into the restaurant and sit at the table. We packed the restaurant bag full of lots of fun activities for him to do at the table. At first we focused on keeping him engaged with activities to establish the restaurant as fun and teach him the options when dining there. His parents would ask him questions about his activities and create a fun experience.

Once he started feeling more comfortable in the space, we created a conversation map for him. He started learning what kinds of things his family would talk about at the table, which we visualized for him on a special place mat. Over time, we faded out the toys and just let him talk with his family. At that point his parents were implementing many more of the language learning activities and strategies. But obviously, to get James to that place, we had to start with getting him comfortable to be in the restaurant at all.

REMEMBER: PLAY IS WORK

Going out to eat is often such a treat for adults, but sometimes it doesn't feel like that for toddlers! It could be a lot of work for them to sit down at the restaurant. Remember that they're having a completely different experience from yours.

CHAPTER 10

OUTSIDE PLAY

Why Outside Play?

Who doesn't like to be outside?

So many of our daily activities with kids are inside, which means their main vocabulary exposure will be for inside activities and things, too. Going outside is not only fun, but it also provides many opportunities for language learning with new vocabulary. You can play with leaves and grass, giving opportunities to use all sorts of new words: crunchy, smooth, dry, cloudy, bugs, and so on.

Being inside the same four walls of the therapy room again and again can get stale. I take my kiddos outside every chance I get. It's good for them, and it's good for me, too! We're also allowed to get messy! We can splash outside. We can be louder. Often, I take the activity we were planning to do inside and move it outside. Even if the children have seen these toys before, there's something novel about seeing them in a different space.

Outside the language learning opportunities, barring a major allergy, it's usually healthy for all of us to spend time outside. Fresh air and sunlight are good for the soul—and the body, too. Regular exposure to sunlight (obviously not to the point of a sunburn) triggers the body to produce vitamin D and is a major factor in hormone regulation. If one of the kids I work with has trouble getting to sleep, I always recommend to the caregiver to spend fifteen to twenty minutes with them outside every day when possible.

What to do? (Separated into verbal levels)

GET PREPARED

This is the time to get prepared for this learning opportunity. Before you collect materials, make sure you've read through the "Get Prepared" section in chapter 5.

Materials Needed

For bubbles:

- ☐ Bubbles (large bubbles with an eight-inch ring): These huge bubbles give us great adjective opportunities: long, small, shiny, oval, go high, go low. We can also describe where the bubbles are going: toward that tree, to that person, flying away. There are lots of gesture opportunities, too!

For obstacle course:

- ☐ Cones
- ☐ Ring
- ☐ Painter's tape
- ☐ Outside chalk
- ☐ Reminder: You do *not* have to buy all these materials to do this activity. But if your child responds very positively to this activity, you could consider buying a few if it seems like it will enhance their experience. I've seen wonderful obstacle courses made with toilet paper finish lines while the kid was weaving in and out of wooden spoons and other kitchen equipment. Cushions from outdoor furniture are also very helpful. I worked with a kiddo whose mom did a lot of craft woodworking, and we used her scraps of wood to build out the barriers and boundary lines for an obstacle course. Use what you have as long as it is a safe material.

Activity Time

Activity 1: Bubbles

Bubbles provide amazing opportunities for both nonverbal and verbal communication. A child can use their hands to indicate the size of a bubble, ranging from a tiny pinch between thumb and forefinger and their arms stretched out wide. There are so many words associated with bubbles, from verbs to adjectives to prepositions.

The activity is self-explanatory: you're going to blow bubbles! But your reactions and how you interact with your child will provide learning opportunities.

PREVERBAL NEXT STEPS

Blowing is great for preverbal kids. They can practice putting their lips together and blowing air through them. They're also learning to use the wand. Body and motor imitation lead to verbal imitation later on!

They can point up or look up, using their hands to communicate where the bubbles are going. You can look up with them, point, and say, "Bubbles up!" Then immediately blow the bubbles in that direction to reinforce that.

They can also watch and mimic your facial expressions and body language.

VERBAL 1 NEXT STEPS

You will add one word to those gestures. They say, "Up!" You say, "Bubbles up!"

They say, "Bubbles." You say, "Big bubbles!"

When you see they're excited, you can help them express that emotion by giving them a word (jump, clap, wow, yay) and modeling an action to use, such as clapping, throwing your arms in the air, and jumping through the bubbles.

A word I hear verbal 1 kiddos say often when they're learning to navigate the bubble wand is "help." This word is so important for many reasons, including avoiding concerning behaviors. When your child asks for help, be sure to celebrate them for doing so *and* help them with the task at hand.

⏭ VERBAL 2 NEXT STEPS

Increase the complexity of what they're saying by adding on verbs and the locations of the bubbles. For example, say, "Bubbles on the ground" or "Bubbles flying high."

If they say, "Help," you can say, "Help me open," or "Help me blow bubbles."

⏭ VERBAL 3 NEXT STEPS

Mix together expressive language, associated words, location words, names, and anything else that organically applies to the bubble experience.

- Bubbles floating up into the air.
- Talk about *who* blew a certain bubble: Grandma blew a big bubble!
- Wow, look at that bubble! It's going so fast!
- Help me open the bubbles, Mom.

Activity 2: Obstacle Course

An obstacle course may sound like it's geared more toward teaching motor skills than teaching language, but that's not true at all! From the moment you start setting up the course (which can be one obstacle if you want it to be simple and small or up to several obstacles), there are so many opportunities for communication. You can narrate and demonstrate: "I'm going to step up onto this block (demonstrate), then I'm going to jump into this circle (demonstrate), then roll across the blanket (demonstrate)."

TO LEARN MORE

To learn more about obstacle courses, I recommend "The Hidden Benefits of Obstacle Courses" available on the Arizona Orthopedic Physical Therapy website.[1]

The skill of physical imitation translates beautifully into expressive language skills. They listen, watch, and do their version.

One of my favorite things about the obstacle course is that it reminds us that their version of anything, whether it's trying to balance on one foot or to say the word "jump," you'll see how their skills are different. It's easier to visualize when these skills are on display in a physical sense and a bit harder when we're thinking about communication and verbal skills. But obstacle courses serve as a reminder to us that they're gradually going to get there.

Here are some things to enhance your obstacle course:

Use visuals. Add visuals at each obstacle, such as a picture of a child doing the action. Stick figures also work! This can increase their independence so you don't have to continue to model the action for them. Just like the diagrams on the side of workout equipment, these visualizations help them translate that action to their own body.

Use the rule of three. Set up the obstacle course, making sure you have their attention. (Having their attention is a huge piece to language learning. They should be looking at you or have their body turned in your direction and listening.) Have them watch you do each part of the obstacle course once. The next time, you help them through it, and the third time is their chance to do it independently.

Start small. Start with one piece if you need to. If you say "Jump in the circle" and they don't understand (this is actually pretty complicated!), that can be challenging. This is an action + an item. So you start small and demonstrate a few times. Have a visual and practice the action while listening to the simple language over and over. As time goes on, you can add more pieces. I've even had verbal 3 kiddos walk me through the obstacle course, which is so much fun!

 PREVERBAL NEXT STEPS

Laughing counts as a gesture! This means they're having fun, which is the perfect opportunity for next steps in language.

For example, let's say you're jumping into a Hula-Hoop that's lying on the ground. You'll demonstrate this for them, saying, "Jump!" as you jump into the hoop. Perhaps they laugh here because you're being silly. Repeat this a couple of times, modeling, "Jump!" but if they just continue to laugh while they jump, that still counts as a vocalization and a movement.

Visuals are huge for preverbal kids. If they love to go outside but they're unable to say "Outside," they can grab a visual to prompt you to let them outside. Teach them to give you the obstacle course items to let you know they want to do that. You'll use one word for three (or so) obstacles. Using visuals absolutely counts as communication.

VERBAL 1 NEXT STEPS

You'll add a word or two to the word they are using to expressively communicate.

If they say, "Jump!" you can say, "Jump in!" or "I jump in!" or "Jump high!"

VERBAL 2 NEXT STEPS

Continue to add complexity to their words. If they say, "I jump high," you say, "I jump high into the circle."

If they say, "I jump in!" you say, "I jump into the circle."

VERBAL 3 NEXT STEPS

Verbal 3 kiddos can verbally walk you through the activity.

You can help them with concepts such as taking turns, who goes next, and so on. You can also prompt them by asking pointed questions, such as "How do I get into the circle?"

You can give them three-step directions. "Grab the Hula-Hoop, put it on the ground, and jump into it!"

Reflection

- What can I do differently to make this easier for everyone next time?
    - Add a visual cue to obstacles.
    - Use an obstacle with fewer steps.
- What communication did I observe? What am I building off next time?

    - Was there a new word or sound to celebrate? A new gesture/sound combination? Did they use a new word for the first time that you can build off next time you have this obstacle out?
    - Continue to celebrate these things next time.
- What skills should we practice more?
- What communication breakdown did we have?

FAQ

He doesn't want to come inside!

Okay, this isn't really a question. But often, when I advise caregivers to take their child outside, they'll say, "Oh, if I take him outside, I won't be able to get him back inside again!"

This is great information for me. Of course, some children just *love* being outside and don't want to stop having fun. For some children, the act of coming inside causes them stress, which needs to be addressed. Either way, it can be very effective to make sure there's something fun waiting for them inside, and make sure you communicate what that is. A visual cue can be very helpful, such as a picture of a popsicle or of their book character.

Always prepare your child from the beginning of going outside by telling them what's going to happen so they don't have anxiety wondering when they'll suddenly be asked to come in. You can tell them, "We're playing outside for thirty minutes, and then we'll go inside and have a popsicle!" "Thirty minutes" won't mean much to them at first, but you've at least created an expectation. Giving a "five more minutes" warning can also help with anxiety.

Another strategy is using a timer to show how much time is left outside. I recommend the Children's Countdown Timer, which is a free smartphone app. It shows an empty circle that fills in as time passes, and at the end of the allotted time, the circle changes to a picture of the next activity. You can change this picture as often as you need to. It can be a popsicle one day and Grandma the next. This is an exceptional visual cue. It also provides them the chance to be more independent with the transition, as they can keep an eye on the timer and know if their outside time is almost up.

We're always outside. What do I do outside to make it a learning opportunity?

I've worked with many children who live in rural settings and have plenty of access to the outdoors. So much so that perhaps it has lost some of its novelty for them and for the caregivers alike.

I worked with one kiddo who was the youngest of five siblings. The kids played in the backyard all day. Mom could supervise them from the kitchen window while she was doing her daily tasks. When the youngest child started displaying delayed communication, she reached out to me.

One of the first things we did was create opportunities for this child to have to communicate with his parents or siblings when he needed something. We zipped up the net around the trampoline so that if he wanted to go on it, he had to communicate to an elder sibling or a parent that he needed something. We also put toys in certain containers so he could "ask" for them. (He was preverbal, so we were looking for pointing or leading us to the object.)

Something else you can do is bring indoor stuff outside. Have a picnic. Read books outside.

You can also rely on the senses. Close your eyes and talk about what you smell and feel. Have your verbal 2 or 3 child use words to tell you about their sensory experiences. Funny ones such as bad smells definitely apply! You can touch the grass, smell the flowers, crush the leaves, and so on. Note the sounds of the birds and the crickets.

"They only want to go on the swing" or "They only want to play in the mulch."

Caregivers often tell me that their child has a singular focus outside, and getting them to do anything else is impossible.

I advise them to try the Grandma's Rule system, making the favorite activity the second thing you do.

For instance, if a kid loves swinging and insists on doing nothing else, you could try to build in opportunities for them to do other things. You can play with this ball together for three minutes and then swing. Maybe the next time, you play ball for three minutes and then play tag for two minutes and then swing. You can use visual cues as well by using the actual object or a photo of it.

I don't have a yard. What can I do?

Utilize any outdoor space you have access to as long as it's safe. You can use a little balcony or a small section of sidewalk. I've seen caregivers make an obstacle course out of painter's tape and sidewalk chalk out in front of their apartment building.

Use natural boundaries as well. Run to the end of that bush. Jump until you get to the fire hydrant. Touch the signpost. These types of things can help you teach boundaries (such as not running into the street) and helpful vocabulary all at once.

Of course, safety is the number one concern, and if you don't feel confident that you can safely navigate these activities with what you have available, you can try these strategies when at a park or when visiting friends or family.

 Case Study

I recently worked with a preverbal kiddo who loved water. His whole body would light up with water play. He wanted to be completely in the water, which wasn't something we could recreate in the therapy room. However, I knew that being able to play with water was huge to his engagement with me and with the materials I presented to him. So anytime the weather was good, we'd go outside. I'd bring dish soap and play with huge bubbles. He didn't have to feel like he could only play in a small way with water. He could pour, splash, and submerge his body.

We were focusing on gestures because he was preverbal, but he ended up surprising me with his first word. I'd always say, "Pour," when I poured water from a cup in front of him. Then one day he said, "Pour!" Which was the beginning of his long list of single words he would produce and later sentences.

We used outside play to harness his interests, which made him incredibly engaged in his learning opportunities.

REMEMBER: PLAY IS WORK

Imitation is hard! This is a skill that sometimes we need to teach directly. Imagine someone's showing you how to swing a golf club and you've never done that before. You have to know where your feet go, where your hands go, how to aim, how to swing—it's a lot!

Adults sometimes take for granted how long we've been living in these bodies and how easy it is to follow directions. We have a lifetime of experience of paying attention. Plus, everybody is different. Some people can watch someone do something for the first time and replicate what they're doing immediately. Others take a bit longer. This is the same for your child.

CHAPTER 11

BOOKS

 Why Books?

When we're little, we learn to read, and when we're older, we read to learn. Books are the most wonderful source of knowledge for humans throughout their lives!

When we read to children, even far before they'll be able to read for themselves, they're mapping out that there's a word/label that goes with things, animals, and people. These sounds feed into preliteracy skills. This is why many SLPs, including myself, are adamant for early intervention. Imitating the sounds in a word is a precursor to preliteracy, and if they fall behind, it can snowball into challenges with learning to read. If they struggle to read when they're young, they could continue to struggle into their school years and even into adulthood. Books also create opportunities to hear words that aren't used in everyday speech.

Research supports that reading five or so books per day to a child starting in infancy sets them up to have a larger vocabulary.[1] It sounds odd that reading to someone who can't understand you or even look at a page would be beneficial, but it is! You aren't just reading something flat and boring to them. You're reading a kid's book and making associated sounds (animal noises or truck noises), changing inflection, and making facial expressions. You're creating a social back-and-forth, sharing a moment together in what is a precursor to conversation.

RESOURCES:
DOLLY PARTON'S IMAGINATION LIBRARY

Dolly Parton's Imagination Library program gives the gift of free books to children every month from birth to age five, depending on funding for various regions. Visit www.imaginationlibrary.com to see if it's available in your town/area. If not, you can communicate with them to see if they can bring the service to your area. The website also has video resources to help parents navigate literacy learning with their children. And it's all free of charge to the child's family.

GET PREPARED

This is the time to get prepared for this learning opportunity. Before you collect materials, make sure you've read through the "Get Prepared" section in chapter 5.

Materials Needed

(This will definitely depend on the child and the book.)

- ☐ A children's book of your choice
- ☐ Manipulatives (for the visual activity discussed below): These include visuals you've printed out, pictures of the characters and locations, items you're matching or sequencing with the child. (If there's a cow in the book, a picture, or a toy cow, they can match to the story.)
- ☐ Puppets (for the visual activity discussed below): This doesn't have to be an actual puppet but just a character they can hold to help act out the action of the story. This also helps with sensory input for their body during the book.
- ☐ Chair or couch (optional): Positioning is important so the child can see the book and your face. You can sit on the floor with them on the couch behind you. Some people create a reading corner in their house with a small chair for the child, raising them up to eye level with the adult.

Activity Time

Activity 1: Adding Visuals

Books are already visual, right?

Well, yes, but a visual in this sense can mean more than looking at the pictures in a book. It can mean letting your child choose the book off the shelf. You can have pictures of the books if they're in a different room or in a container. If a child is looking for it in a big stack, they may not be able to tell you what they're looking for, but they could select it based on a picture.

I love the book *Monster Emotions* for its potential visual cues. I have laminated pictures of many of the pages, where different monsters act out different emotions, and use these images in a variety of ways, all the way from emotional gestures to talking about emotions in a storytelling way.

I've found that by looking at a picture from within the book, or real items that look like the characters in the book can keep our kiddos attention on the language learning opportunities. When you've managed to read a book with them several times, this is a perfect opportunity for them to begin to look at the book on their own and walk you through it.

Other visuals you can add are as follows:

A puppet. This doesn't have to be an actual puppet. It can be a stuffed animal that you're pretending is reading the book. It could be a puppet, though, made from a sock or your hand in a paper bag. As long as it's creating a new dynamic to the reading experience, go for it. I've had fun with some kids by printing out pictures of the characters in a certain book, then taping them to the paper bags and each of us getting to "act out" the story.

Movement. Notice when you can add a gesture or movement into the book. If there's an elephant, you can use your forearm like a trunk and make an elephant sound. Or for a lion, put your hands up like claws. These small things add dimension to the reading experience and can be a welcome relief for kiddos who don't naturally love reading. They get a moment to refocus and engage with the story in the form of movement. If a character is running, pump arms by your sides and act winded. Or jump up and run in a circle and let the kid do the same. For very active kiddos, adding this movement can be essential to get wiggles out before coming back.

PREVERBAL NEXT STEPS

Work on building on gestures for emotions and noises for animals and asking them to point to different characters on the page.

VERBAL 1 NEXT STEPS

Encourage them to label visuals with single words (pointing to the sad monster and saying, "Sad").

Or you can have them imitate "monster."

Coming back to the SPOT goals, I like to focus on a specific word to be our goal for the activity.

Think about what would be the best word for them to learn to use. If you're reading the *Monster Emotions*, maybe you want them to say "Mad." So you point to the mad monster and say, "Mad." Model it a few times to see if they will mimic you.

VERBAL 2 NEXT STEPS

Adding a word to what they say, such as "He's sad" or "I'm sad" (assuming the kid already says, "Sad"). Always build off what they're giving us. Add adjectives, nouns, and pronouns onto the word they used.

VERBAL 3 NEXT STEPS

There's a visual activity I love to do with *Monster Emotions* for verbal 3 kiddos. I read the book with them, get out printouts I have of images of the different monsters, and see if the child can put the emotions in order the way they occur in the book.

Then they can talk about each monster. They can even do this part without ever reading the book.

Activity 2: Sing a Nursery Rhyme

Use the images and words in the book to inspire a bit of singing, much like in the bath time activity. If there's a sun in the sky, you could sing, "Mr. Sun, Sun, Mr. Golden Sun," while adding movement with your hands or arms like a rising sun.

Especially for kids who love movement and music, you're now incorporating their two favorite things into this activity that could seem boring otherwise. If someone's sleeping in the picture, you can sing, "Are You Sleeping?" and put your hands under your cheek and close your eyes, pretending to be asleep.

If your child responds well to this activity, you could get some books that are based on nursery rhymes, so the singing is built in. "Wheels on the Bus" is a particularly good song to incorporate movement because it is about movement! There are many picture book renditions of this song.

You can make up your own songs as well. Sometimes, it's more fun to make up your own words while using the tune to a famous nursery rhyme. Switching the words up will get their attention, but it might also throw them off. If your child wouldn't like you changing the words, you can always pull up an audio version of the song online and listen to it together, both singing along or dancing.

PREVERBAL NEXT STEPS

Have them mimic (some of) the gestures you're using, such as the sun overhead or the sleeping person. Maybe they'll vocalize as well, such as the snoring sound that goes with the sleeping person or the "Ahhhhhh . . ." yawn of just waking up.

VERBAL 1 NEXT STEPS

Have a goal of them singing one or two words consistently throughout the song, and use gestures with the song such as pretending to sleep. Maybe try to say "Sleep" while doing the gesture.

VERBAL 2 AND 3 NEXT STEPS

Continue to build off the words they're already singing, such as saying, "I am sleeping" or "Snoring loud!" Keep going, and eventually they'll know the whole song!

Activity 3: Storytelling

This activity goes both ways, depending on the verbal level. You can tell them a story, or they can tell you a story.

Start by telling them a story. It could be about something that you enjoyed in your childhood. You could completely make it up. Or you could recap an episode of one of their favorite shows or one of the books you've recently read together.

You can add a visual to this story. Add a stuffed animal or a picture of you from your childhood. It can be anything as long as it's something tangible that takes the place of the book while storytelling.

If applicable, have your child retell their favorite story. (Try to only be a listener—this can be hard for adults to only listen. Don't worry about correcting them or adding anything to what they are saying. Just listen until they obviously need help finding a word or if it's your turn to speak.)

 PREVERBAL NEXT STEPS

I've had preverbal kiddos tell me stories in gestures and facial expressions. It was really cute. While the kiddo was using gestures and facial expressions, I narrated my interpretations aloud. This is the foundation of sharing information back-and-forth and conversation skills.

 VERBAL 1 NEXT STEPS

You'll probably need to fill in words for them as they tell you a very brief story. It is still is a great learning opportunity. They're getting exposure to additional language and the social aspect of telling a story together.

You can also use props to help!

 VERBAL 2 NEXT STEPS

Similar to verbal 1, but the caregiver fills in fewer words.

 VERBAL 3 NEXT STEPS

Now we have more freedom to be creative. You might make up a story together completely from imagination. You can ask questions such as "What does he like to eat?" or "Does he have a best friend?" to prompt them.

Reflection

- How did it go?
- What can I do differently to make this easier for everyone next time?
    - Add a visual cue.
    - Add in movement.
- What communication did I observe? What am I building off next time?
    - Was there a new word or sound to celebrate? A new gesture/sound combination? Did they use a new word for the first time that you can build off next time you have this obstacle out?
    - Continue to celebrate these things next time.
- What skills should we practice more?
- What communication breakdown did we have?
- Did I ask too many questions (especially for a kid with a disability)?
- Was this activity longer than it has been in the past?
    - What made it longer?

FAQ

What do I do if my child doesn't enjoy books?

Do they like movement? Think of ways to incorporate movement. If they like music, use their favorite songs. If they like touching things and kinesthetic activities, use books with different textures.

This is usually the first way I get them interested in books. They're engaging with a book positively through touch, and you can build off that. Gradually build toward reading the story.

REMEMBER: PLAY IS WORK

This chapter-by-chapter reminder emphasizes that even if these activities seem easy to you, they're work for your child, even if you make it fun! Learning is hard work.

Do you like getting quizzed incessantly by other adults? No! Kids don't like that, either. We don't want everything we do to entail quizzing the kid incessantly. Adults sometimes think that this is the only way to teach or that it's a fun back-and-forth, but the child gets tired of having to come up with answers to all these questions. I'm not saying *not* to ask questions; rather I suggest being pointed with your questions and making sure to stop after a reasonable number. If you want to teach the word "who," then you can ask a few "who" questions, such as "Who is that?" or "Who is [name of character]?" If the questions are too hard, the kid might get frustrated.

PUTTING IT ALL TOGETHER

This book is a labor of love for so many reasons. I've worked with many amazing families over the course of my career and gotten to share in their joy as they've made progress communicating with their little one and experiencing first words that lead to sentences and beyond. I've gotten to roll around on the floor, smash Play-Doh, blow bubbles, and hear caregivers being called "mom or dad" for the first time. It never gets old. Every kiddo I've worked with has changed me a little bit.

But something happened to me during the writing of this book. In March 2024 I became a mother for the first time.

Though I've witnessed hundreds of parents get to hear their child's first words, I've never been truly in their shoes. I wrote this book for every caregiver and parent I've ever worked with, all the ones I haven't yet, and their amazing kiddos who are doing the hard work of learning to communicate. I started this book while pregnant, wrote the bulk of it on maternity leave, and finished it when I could block off a couple of hours here and there between being a mom and my work. Now as I put the finishing touches on it, I'm excited to realize that had I never become a speech-language pathologist and written this book, this book would be for *me*. I'm that new parent of a preverbal child who is on his way to his first words. I don't know when that day will be, but I know it will be the most exciting day of my life.

No matter how old your kiddo is or what verbal level they are, I hope you found something helpful in this book. *Path for Words: Five-Minute Language Learning Activities for Children* builds targeted language-learning opportunities into the daily routines you already do with your kiddo, which can help increase the complexity of their language, help avoid communication breakdowns, and, of course, teach them new words!

In part 1 we discussed the importance of early intervention. If you suspect your child may have a developmental difference, don't wait for months to see a speech therapist. Those precious months can be crucial to your child's ability to communicate with you. Because communication breakdowns are often at the root of concerning behaviors, early intervention can also help you learn to communicate effectively with your kiddo no matter their verbal level, which often helps to avoid concerning behaviors.

We learned about the developmental milestones and how to monitor them. I encouraged you to expose your child to other languages. If you speak another language at home, please seek out speech therapists who empower you to raise a bilingual or multilingual child. There is no evidence that denying them your native language or the language of your family will help them learn English more effectively.

We talked about concerning behaviors and how helping your child communicate at a higher level can help avoid them. We also discussed the very common idea that a child will grow out of them naturally, when that is not always true. A two-year-old biting and kicking may not seem like a big deal, but if they are still doing that at ten, it will be much harder to navigate. Just like seeing a speech therapist at the earliest signs of a learning difference, it is a good idea to seek out help if your kiddo is repeatedly displaying concerning behaviors.

Should you seek out an SLP, I spent a chapter describing what you can do to get the most out of your sessions. (Reading this book and reinforcing your child's language learning at home is a *great* way to get the most out of their sessions!)

In part 2 we broke down the verbal levels and the SPOT strategies of teaching, which appeared in each activity in the book. From there, I led you through multiple activities that fit right in with your daily routines: bath time, diaper changes, snack time, restaurants, outside play, and reading books. Though the routines and locations are different, there is a huge main theme to effective language teaching, which is to build onto your child's existing strengths (and learn to identify those, too).

If you haven't already, start by identifying your child's verbal level. Then pick an activity you think would be fun for you and your family. Get your pens ready for those checklists, and go have fun teaching your kiddo the beautiful skill of language.

I appreciate you taking this journey with me. If you'd like additional resources, such as how to break these activities down specifically for your child, please reach out to the Path for Words community at our website, www.pathforwords.com. We also create fun flowcharts on our social media pages. Follow us on Instagram at @pathforwords.

NOTES

INTRODUCTION

1 Fern Sussman, *More Than Words: Helping Parents Promote Communication and Social Skills in Children with Autism Spectrum Disorder* (Hanen Centre, 1999).

2 "Albert Mehrabian," UCLA Department of Psychology, August 13, 2021, https://www.psych.ucla.edu/faculty-page/mehrab/.

CHAPTER 1

1 Irla Lee Zimmerman et al., "Preschool Language Scales | Fifth Edition," Pearson, 2019, https://www.pearsonassessments.com/store/usassessments/en/Store/Professional-Assessments/Speech-%26-Language/Preschool-Language-Scales-%7C-Fifth-Edition/p/100000233.html.

2 "Identify the Signs of Communication Disorders," American Speech-Language-Hearing Association, 2013, https://identifythesigns.org/.

3 "Learn the Signs. Act Early," Centers for Disease Control and Prevention, last reviewed May 22, 2024, https://www.cdc.gov/ncbddd/actearly/.

4 "Developing Early Literacy: Report of the National Early Literacy Panel," National Institute for Literacy, 2008, https://lincs.ed.gov/publications/pdf/NELPReport09.pdf.

5 "Creation of ASHA's Developmental Milestones," American Speech-Language-Hearing Association, 2024, https://www.asha.org/public/developmental-milestones/creation-of-ashas-developmental-milestones/.

6 "Mehrabian's Communication Study," Changing Minds, 2019, http://changingminds.org/explanations/behaviors/body_language/mehrabian.htm.

7 Susan Goldin-Meadow, "Gesture as a Window onto Communicative Abilities: Implications for Diagnosis and Intervention," *Perspectives on Language Learning and Education* 22, no. 2 (2015): 50–60, https://doi.org/10.1044/lle22.2.50.

8 Courtney E. Venker et al., "Increasing Verbal Responsiveness in Parents of Children with Autism: A Pilot Study," *Autism* 16, no. 6 (2011): 568–85, https://doi.org/10.1177/1362361311413396.

9 Elizabeth Kirk et al., "To Sign or Not to Sign? The Impact of Encouraging Infants to Gesture on Infant Language and Maternal Mind-Mindedness," *Child Development* 84, no. 2 (2012): 574–90. https://doi.org/10.1111/j.1467-8624.2012.01874.x.

10 "16 by 16 Lookbooks," First Words Project, n.d., https://firstwordsproject.com/16-by-16-lookbooks/.

11 "The Ultimate Guide to Speech Intelligibility in Toddlers," Playing Speech, August 10, 2023, https://www.playingspeech.com/blog/toddlersandspeechsounddisorders-bsf75.

CHAPTER 2

1 "American Sign Language," National Institute on Deafness and Other Communication Disorders, March 6, 2019, https://www.nidcd.nih.gov/health/american-sign-language.

2 "Learning More than One Language," American Speech-Language-Hearing Association, n.d., https://www.asha.org/public/speech/development/learning-more-than-one-language/.

3 Tracy Trautner, "Advantages of a Bilingual Brain," Michigan State University Extension, January 28, 2019, https://www.canr.msu.edu/news/advantages_of_a_bilingual_brain#:~:text=Between%20the%20ages%20of%200.

4 Janet F. Werker and Richard C. Tees, "Speech Perception as a Window for Understanding Plasticity and Commitment in Language Systems of the Brain," *Developmental Psychobiology* 46, no. 3 (2005): 233–51, https://doi.org/10.1002/dev.20060.

5 Toms Voits et al., "The Effects of Bilingualism on Hippocampal Volume in Ageing Bilinguals," *Brain Structure and Function* 227, no. 3 (2022): 979-94, https://doi.org/10.1007/s00429-021-02436-z.

6 Olumide A. Olulade et al., "Neuroanatomical Evidence in Support of the Bilingual Advantage Theory," *Cerebral Cortex* 26, no. 7 (2015): 3196–204, https://doi.org/10.1093/cercor/bhv152.

7 Barbara Zurer Pearson, *Raising a Bilingual Child: A Step-By-Step Guide for Parents* (2023).

8 Lauren Lowry Hanen, "Bilingualism in Young Children: Separating Fact from Fiction," Hanen Centre, 2016, https://www.hanen.org/helpful-info/articles/bilingualism-in-young-children--separating-fact-fr.aspx.

9 Sandra Aamodt and Sam Wang, *Welcome to Your Child's Brain: How the Mind Grows from Conception to College* (Bloomsbury, 2012).

10 "Starter Guide: Important Foundational Principles," Multilingual Learning Toolkit, n.d., https://www.multilinguallearningtoolkit.org/starter-guide/.

11 "FAQ: Raising Bilingual Children | Linguistic Society of America," Linguistic Society of America, 2019, https://www.linguisticsociety.org/resource/faq-raising-bilingual-children.

12 National Academies of Sciences, Engineering, and Medicine, *Promoting the Educational Success of Children and Youth Learning English: Promising Futures* (National Academies Press, n.d.).

13 M. Pilar Trelles and Karen Castro, "Bilingualism in Autism Spectrum Disorder: Finding Meaning in Translation," *Journal of the American Academy of Child and Adolescent Psychiatry* 58, no. 11 (2019): 1035–37, https://doi.org/10.1016/j.jaac.2019.05.027.

14 Ellen Bialystok and Janet F. Werker, "Editorial: The Systematic Effects of Bilingualism on Children's Development," *Developmental Science* 20, no. 1 (2016): e12535, https://doi.org/10.1111/desc.12535.

CHAPTER 3

1 Glen Dunlap and Michelle Duda, "Using Functional Communication Training to Replace Challenging Behavior," Center on the Social and Emotional Foundations for Early Learning, July 2004, http://csefel.vanderbilt.edu/briefs/wwb11.pdf.

2 Bob McMurray, "Defusing the Childhood Vocabulary Explosion," *Science* 317, no. 5838 (2007): 631–31, https://doi.org/10.1126/science.1144073.

3 Dunlap and Duda, "Functional Communication Training."

4 "Definition of Communication," American Speech-Language-Hearing Association, 2013, https://www.asha.org/NJC/Definition-of-Communication-and-Appropriate-Targets/.

5 "What Is Speech? What Is Language?" American Speech-Language-Hearing Association, 2024, https://www.asha.org/public/speech/development/speech-and-language/.

6 "Challenging Behavior as Communication," Evidence-Based Instructional Practices, n.d., https://ebip.vkcsites.org/challenging-behavior-as-communication/.

7 Julia L. Evans and Holly K. Craig, "Language Sample Collection and Analysis," *Journal of Speech, Language, and Hearing Research* 35, no. 2 (1992): 343–53, https://doi.org/10.1044/jshr.3502.343.

8 "Pyramid Model," Center on the Social and Emotional Foundations for Early Learning, n.d., https://csefel.vanderbilt.edu/csefelindex.html.

9 “Collection: Book Nook,” National Center for Pyramid Model Innovations, 2022, https://challengingbehavior.org/collection/book-nook/.

CHAPTER 4

1 “Naturalistic Intervention: Steps for Implementation,” National Professional Development Center on Autism Spectrum Disorders, 2010, https://csesa.fpg.unc.edu/sites/csesa.fpg.unc.edu/files/ebpbriefs/Naturalistic_Steps.pdf.

2 Ashlyn L. Smith et al., “AAC and Families: Dispelling Myths and Empowering Parents,” *Perspectives of the ASHA Special Interest Groups* 1, no. 12 (2016): 10–20, https://doi.org/10.1044/persp1.sig12.10.

CHAPTER 5

1 National Professional Development Center on Autism Spectrum Disorders, “Naturalistic Intervention: Steps for Implementation.”

2 “Screen Time Guidelines,” American Academy of Pediatrics, 2024, https://www.aap.org/en/patient-care/media-and-children/center-of-excellence-on-social-media-and-youth-mental-health/qa-portal/qa-portal-library/qa-portal-library-questions/screen-time-guidelines/?srsltid=AfmBOop3ivCOhZjD5MgQ4lcnEWhL7T5ZW6yJGsJ1nJgXGuz2rzLxDeuL.

3 Nancy Swigert, *The Early Intervention Kit* (LinguiSystems, 2004).

4 Housson Center Staff, “Grandma’s Rule; Cultivating Motivation,” Housson Center, May 29, 2020, https://thehoussoncenter.com/grandmas-rule-cultivating-motivation/.

5 Leanne Page, *Parenting with Science: Behavior Analysis Saves Mom’s Sanity* (BCBAtoday, 2015).

CHAPTER 6

1 "10 Activities to Work on Joint Attention," Clubhouse, June 2, 2021, https://www.communicationclubhouse.com/blog/activities-for-joint-attention/#:~:text=Joint%20attention%20is%20when%20a.

2 "Pyramid Model," Center on the Social and Emotional Foundations for Early Learning.

CHAPTER 8

1 Keith E. Williams and Laura J. Seiverling, *Broccoli Boot Camp: Basic Training for Parents of Selective Eaters* (Special Needs Collection, 2018).

CHAPTER 9

1 "Augmentative and Alternative Communication (AAC)," American Speech-Language-Hearing Association, 2024, https://www.asha.org/public/speech/disorders/aac/.

CHAPTER 10

1 "The Hidden Benefits of Obstacle Courses," Arizona Orthopedic Physical Therapy," April 25, 2024, https://azopt.net/the-hidden-benefits-of-obstacle-courses/#:~:text=Obstacle%20courses%20are%20a%20great.

CHAPTER 11

1 Adam M. Franks et al., "Parental Reading to Infants Improves Language Score: A Rural Family Medicine Intervention," *Journal of the American Board of Family Medicine* 35, no. 6 (2022): 1156–62, https://doi.org/10.3122/jabfm.2022.220064r2.

ABOUT THE AUTHOR

Marie Martinez is a dually certified professional in behavior analysis and pediatric speech-language pathology, with extensive clinical experience. As one of the few experts in both fields, Marie has contributed to research on parent coaching, asynchronous family supports, and family outreach. An invited presenter, she frequently shares insights on integrating speech and language strategies with early childhood best practices. In addition to her clinical work, Marie serves as the professional development manager for the American Speech-Language and Hearing Telepractice Special Interest Group, advancing the field of telepractice. Marie is also the founder of the Path for Words program, which supports caregivers in creating speech and language opportunities for their children's development. Passionate about supporting families, Marie combines academic expertise with practical experience to empower caregivers and enhance children's development. A dedicated professional and a mother, she is committed to fostering lasting positive change in the lives of families.